Harvard Business Review

ON

BUSINESS MODEL INNOVATION

THE HARVARD BUSINESS REVIEW PAPERBACK SERIES

The series is designed to bring today's managers and professionals the fundamental information they need to stay competitive in a fast-moving world. From the preeminent thinkers whose work has defined an entire field to the rising stars who will redefine the way we think about business, here are the leading minds and landmark ideas that have established the *Harvard Business Review* as required reading for ambitious businesspeople in organizations around the globe.

Other books in the series:

Harvard Business Review McKinsey Award Winners

Harvard Business Review Interviews with CEOs

Harvard Business Review on Advances in Strategy

Harvard Business Review on Appraising Employee Performance

Harvard Business Review on Becoming a High Performance Manager

Harvard Business Review on Brand Management

Harvard Business Review on Breakthrough Leadership

Harvard Business Review on Breakthrough Thinking

Harvard Business Review on Bringing Your Whole Self to Work

Harvard Business Review on Building Personal and Organizational Resilience

Harvard Business Review on the Business Value of IT

Harvard Business Review on CEO Succession

Harvard Business Review on Change

Harvard Business Review on Collaborating Across Silos

Harvard Business Review on Compensation

Harvard Business Review on Corporate Ethics

Harvard Business Review on Corporate Governance

Harvard Business Review on Corporate Responsibility

Other books in the series (continued):

Harvard Business Review

ON

BUSINESS MODEL

INNOVATION

A HARVARD BUSINESS REVIEW PAPERBACK

Library-of-Congress Cataloging information forthcoming

ISBN: 978-1-4221-3342-2

Table of Contents

Harvard
Business
Review

ON

BUSINESS MODEL INNOVATION

Why Business Models Matter

JOAN MAGRETTA

Executive Summary

"BUSINESS MODEL" was one of the great buzzwords of the Internet boom. A company didn't need a strategy, a special competence, or even any customers—all it needed was a Web-based business model that promised wild profits in some distant, ill-defined future. Many people—investors, entrepreneurs, and executives alike—fell for the fantasy and got burned. And as the inevitable counter-reaction played out, the concept of the business model fell out of fashion nearly as quickly as the .com appendage itself.

That's a shame. As Joan Magretta explains, a good business model remains essential to every successful organization, whether it's a new venture or an established player. To help managers apply

1

the concept successfully, she defines what a business model is and how it complements a smart competitive strategy.

Business models are, at heart, stories that explain how enterprises work. Like a good story, a robust business model contains precisely delineated characters, plausible motivations, and a plot that turns on an insight about value. It answers certain questions: Who is the customer? How do we make money? What underlying economic logic explains how we can deliver value to customers at an appropriate cost?

Every viable organization is built on a sound business model, but a business model isn't a strategy, even though many people use the terms interchangeably. Business models describe, as a system, how the pieces of a business fit together. But they don't factor in one critical dimension of performance: competition. That's the job of strategy.

Illustrated with examples from companies like American Express, EuroDisney, Wal-Mart, and Dell Computer, this article clarifies the concepts of business models and strategy, which are fundamental to every company's performance.

"Business model" was one of the great buzzwords of the Internet boom, routinely invoked, as the writer Michael Lewis put it, "to glorify all manner of half-baked plans." A company didn't need a strategy, or a special competence, or even any customers—all it needed was a Web-based business model that promised wild profits in some distant, ill-defined future. Many people—investors, entrepreneurs, and executives alike—bought the fantasy and got burned. And as the inevitable counterreaction played out, the concept of the business model fell out of fashion nearly as quickly as the .com appendage itself.

That's a shame. For while it's true that a lot of capital was raised to fund flawed business models, the fault lies not with the concept of the business model but with its distortion and misuse. A good business model remains essential to every successful organization, whether it's a new venture or an established player. But before managers can apply the concept, they need a simple working definition that clears up the fuzziness associated with the term.

Telling a Good Story

The word "model" conjures up images of white boards covered with arcane mathematical formulas. Business models, though, are anything but arcane. They are, at heart, stories—stories that explain how enterprises work. A good business model answers Peter Drucker's age-old questions: Who is the customer? And what does the customer value? It also answers the fundamental questions every manager must ask: How do we make money in this business? What is the underlying economic logic that explains how we can deliver value to customers at an appropriate cost?

Consider the story behind one of the most successful business models of all time: that of the traveler's check. During a European vacation in 1892, J.C. Fargo, the president of American Express, had a hard time translating his letters of credit into cash. "The moment I got off the beaten path," he said on his return, "they were no more use than so much wet wrapping paper. If the president of American Express has that sort of trouble, just think what ordinary travelers face. Something has got to be done about it."[1] What American Express did was to create the traveler's check—and from that innovation evolved a robust business model with all the elements of a good story: precisely delineated characters, plausible motivations, and a plot that turns on an insight about value.

The story was straightforward for customers. In exchange for a small fee, travelers could buy both peace of mind (the checks were insured against loss and theft) and convenience (they were very widely accepted). Merchants also played a key role in the tale. They accepted the checks because they trusted the American Express name, which was like a universal letter of credit, and because, by accepting them, they attracted more customers. The more other merchants accepted the checks, the stronger any individual merchant's motivation became not to be left out.

As for American Express, it had discovered a riskless business, because customers always paid cash for the checks. Therein lies the twist to the plot, the underlying economic logic that turned what would have been an unremarkable operation into a money machine. The twist was *float*. In most businesses, costs precede revenues: Before anyone can buy your product, you've got to build it and pay for it. The traveler's check turned the cycle of debt and risk on its head. Because people paid for the checks before (often long before) they used them, American Express was getting something banks had long enjoyed—the equivalent of an interest-free loan from its customers. Moreover, some of the checks were never cashed, giving the company an extra windfall.

As this story shows, a successful business model represents a better way than the existing alternatives. It may offer more value to a discrete group of customers. Or it may completely replace the old way of doing things and become the standard for the next generation of entrepreneurs to beat. Nobody today would head off on vacation armed with a suitcase full of letters of credit. Fargo's business model changed the rules of the game, in this case, the economics of travel. By eliminating the fear of being robbed and the hours spent trying to get cash in a strange city, the checks removed a significant barrier to travel, helping many more people to take many more trips. Like all really powerful business models, this one didn't just shift existing revenues among companies; it created new, incremental demand. Traveler's checks remained the preferred method for taking money abroad for decades, until a new technology—the automated teller machine—granted travelers even greater convenience.

Creating a business model is, then, a lot like writing a new story. At some level, all new stories are variations on old ones, reworkings of the universal themes underlying all human experience. Similarly, all new business models are variations on the generic value chain underlying all businesses. Broadly speaking, this chain has two parts. Part one includes all the activities associated with making something: designing it, purchasing raw materials, manufacturing, and so on. Part two includes all the activities associated with selling something: finding and reaching customers, transacting a sale, distributing the product or delivering the service. A new business model's plot may turn on designing a new product for an unmet need, as it did with the traveler's check. Or it may turn on a process innovation, a better way of making or selling or distributing an already proven product or service.

Think about the simple business that direct-marketing pioneer Michael Bronner created in 1980 when he was a junior at Boston University. Like his classmates, Bronner had occasionally bought books of discount coupons for local stores and restaurants. Students paid a small fee for the coupon books. But Bronner had a better idea. Yes, the books created value for students, but they had the potential to create much more value for merchants, who stood to gain by increasing their sales of pizza and haircuts. Bronner realized that the key to unlocking that potential was wider distribution—putting a coupon book in every student's backpack.

That posed two problems. First, as Bronner well knew, students were often strapped for cash. Giving the books away for free would solve that problem. Second, Bronner needed to get the books to students at a cost that wouldn't eat up his profits. So he made a clever proposal to the dean of Boston University's housing department: Bronner would assemble the coupon books and deliver them in bulk to the housing department, and the department could distribute them free to every dorm on campus. This would make the department look good in the eyes of the students, a notoriously tough crowd to please. The dean agreed.

Now Bronner could make an even more interesting proposal to neighborhood business owners. If they agreed to pay a small fee to appear in the new book, their coupons would be seen by all 14,000 residents of BU's dorms. Bronner's idea took off. Before long, he had extended the concept to other campuses, then to downtown office buildings. Eastern Exclusives, his first company, was born. His innovation wasn't the coupon book but his business model; it worked because he had insight into the motivations of three sets of characters: students, merchants, and school administrators.

Tying Narrative to Numbers

The term "business model" first came into widespread use with the advent of the personal computer and the spreadsheet. Before the spreadsheet, business planning usually meant producing a single, base-case forecast. At best, you did a little sensitivity analysis around the projection. The spreadsheet ushered in a much more analytic approach to planning because every major line item could be pulled apart, its components and subcomponents analyzed and tested. You could ask what-if questions about the critical assumptions on which your business depended—for example, what if customers are more price-sensitive than we thought?—and with a few keystrokes, you could see how any change would play out on every aspect of the whole. In other words, you could model the behavior of a business.

This was something new. Before the personal computer changed the nature of business planning, most successful business models, like Fargo's, were created more by accident than by design and forethought. The business model became clear only after the fact. By enabling companies to tie their marketplace insights much more tightly to the resulting economics—to link their assumptions about how people would behave to the numbers of a pro forma P&L—spreadsheets made it possible to model businesses *before* they were launched.

Of course, a spreadsheet is only as good as the assumptions that go into it. Once an enterprise starts operating, the underlying assumptions of its model—about both motivations and economics—are subjected to continuous testing in the marketplace. And success often hinges on management's ability to tweak, or even overhaul, the model on the fly. When EuroDisney opened its Paris theme park in 1992, it borrowed the business model that had worked so well in Disney's U.S. parks. Europeans, the company thought, would spend roughly the same amount of time and money per visit as Americans did on food, rides, and souvenirs.

Each of Disney's assumptions about the revenue side of the business turned out to be wrong. Europeans did not, for example, graze all day long at the park's various restaurants the way Americans did. Instead, they all expected to be seated at precisely the same lunch or dinner hour, which overloaded the facilities and created long lines of frustrated patrons. Because of those miscalculations, EuroDisney was something of a disaster in its early years. It became a success only after a dozen or so of the key elements in its business model were changed, one by one.

When managers operate consciously from a model of how the entire business system will work, every decision, initiative, and measurement provides valuable feedback. Profits are important not only for their own sake but also because they tell you whether your model is working. If you fail to achieve the results you expected, you reexamine your model, as EuroDisney did. Business modeling is, in this sense, the managerial equivalent of the scientific method—you start with a hypothesis, which you then test in action and revise when necessary.

Two Critical Tests

When business models don't work, it's because they fail either the narrative test (the story doesn't make sense) or the numbers test (the P&L doesn't add up). The business model of on-line grocers, for instance, failed the numbers test. The grocery industry has very thin margins to begin with, and on-line merchants like Webvan incurred new costs for marketing, service, delivery, and technology. Since customers weren't willing to pay significantly more for groceries bought on-line than in stores, there was no way the math could work. Internet grocers had plenty of company. Many ventures in the first wave of electronic commerce failed simply because the basic business math was flawed.

Other business models failed the narrative test. Consider the rapid rise and fall of Priceline Webhouse Club. This was an offshoot of Priceline.com, the company that introduced name-your-own pricing to the purchase of airline tickets. Wall Street's early enthusiasm encouraged CEO Jay Walker to extend his concept to groceries and gasoline.

Here's the story Walker tried to tell. Via the Web, millions of consumers would tell him how much they wanted to pay for, say, a jar of peanut butter. Consumers could specify the price but not the brand, so they might end up with Jif or they might end up with Skippy. Webhouse would then aggregate the bids and go to companies like P&G and Bestfoods and try to make a deal: Take 50 cents off the price of your peanut butter, and we'll order a million jars this week. Webhouse wanted to be a power broker for individual consumers: Representing millions of shoppers, it would negotiate discounts and then pass on the savings to its customers, taking a fee in the process.

What was wrong with the story? It assumed that companies like P&G, Kimberly-Clark, and Exxon wanted to play this game. Think about that for a minute. Big consumer companies have spent decades and billions of dollars building brand loyalty. The Webhouse model teaches consumers to buy on price alone. So why would the manufacturers want to help Webhouse undermine both their prices and the brand identities they'd worked so hard to build? They wouldn't. The story just didn't make sense. To be a power broker, Webhouse needed a huge base of loyal customers. To get those customers, it first needed to deliver discounts. Since the consumer product companies refused to play, Webhouse had to pay for those discounts out of its own pocket. A few hundred million dollars later, in October 2000, it ran out of cash—and out of investors who still believed the story.

In case anyone thinks that Internet entrepreneurs have a monopoly on flawed business models, think again. We tend to forget about ideas that don't pan out, but business history is littered with them. In the 1980s, the one-stop financial supermarket was a business model that fired the imagination of many executives—but Sears, to cite one example, discovered that its customers just didn't get the connection between power tools and annuities. In the 1990s, Silicon Graphics invested hundreds of millions of dollars in interactive television, but it was unable to find real customers who were as enchanted by the technology as the engineers who invented it. Ultimately, models like these fail because they are built on faulty assumptions about customer behavior. They are solutions in search of a problem.

The irony about the slipshod use of the concept of business models is that when used correctly, it actually forces managers to think rigorously about their businesses. A business model's great strength as a planning tool is that it focuses attention on how all the elements of the system fit into a working whole. It's no surprise that, even during the Internet boom, executives who grasped the basics of business model thinking were in a better position to lead the winners. Meg Whitman, for example, joined eBay in its early days because she was struck by what she described as "the emotional connection between eBay users and the site."[2] The way people behaved was an early indicator of the potential power of the eBay brand. Whitman also realized that eBay, unlike many Internet businesses that were being created, simply "couldn't be done off-line." In other words, Whitman—a seasoned executive—saw a compelling, coherent narrative with the potential to be translated into a profitable business.

Whitman has remained attentive to the psychology and the economics that draw collectors, bargain hunters, community seekers, and small-business people to eBay. Its auction model succeeds not just because the Internet lowers the cost of connecting vast numbers of buyers and sellers but also because eBay has made decisions about the scope of its activities that result in an appropriate cost structure. After an auction, eBay leaves it to the sellers and buyers to work out the logistics of payment and shipping. The company never takes possession of the goods or carries any inventory. It incurs no transportation costs. It bears no credit risk. And it has none of the overhead that would come with those activities.

What About Strategy?

Every viable organization is built on a sound business model, whether or not its founders or its managers conceive of what they do in those terms. But a business model isn't the same thing as a strategy, even though many people use the terms interchangeably today. Business models describe, as a system, how the pieces of a business fit together. But they don't factor in one critical dimension of performance: competition. Sooner or later—and it is usually sooner—every enterprise runs into competitors. Dealing with that reality is strategy's job.

A competitive strategy explains how you will do better than your rivals. And doing better, by definition, means being different. Organizations achieve superior performance when they are unique, when they do something no other business does in ways that no other business can duplicate. When you cut away the jargon, that's what strategy is all about—how you are going to do better by being different. The logic is straightforward: When all companies offer the same products and services to the same customers by performing the same kinds of activities, no company will prosper. Customers will benefit, at least in the short term, while head-to-head competition drives prices down to a point where returns are inadequate. It was precisely this kind of competition—destructive competition, to use Michael Porter's term—that did in many Internet retailers, whether they were selling pet supplies, drugs, or toys. Too many fledgling companies rushed to market with identical business models and no strategies to differentiate themselves in terms of which customers and markets to serve, what products and services to offer, and what kinds of value to create.

To see the distinction between a strategy and a business model, you need only look at Wal-Mart. You might think that the giant retailer's success was a result of pioneering a new business model, but that's not the case. When Sam Walton opened his first Wal-Mart in 1962 in the hamlet of Rogers, Arkansas, the discount-retailing business model had been around for a few years. It had emerged in the mid- 1950s, when a slew of industry pioneers (now long forgotten) began to apply supermarket logic to the sale of general merchandise. Supermarkets had been educating customers since the 1930s about the value of giving up personal service in exchange for lower food prices, and the new breed of retailers saw that they could adapt the basic story line of the supermarket to clothing, appliances, and a host of other consumer goods. The idea was to offer lower prices than conventional department stores by slashing costs. And so the basic business model for discount retailing took shape: First, strip away the department store's physical amenities such as the carpeting and the chandeliers. Second, configure the stores to handle large numbers of shoppers efficiently. And third, put fewer salespeople on the floor and rely on customers to serve themselves. Do those things well, and you could offer low prices and still make money.

Walton heard about the new discount stores, visited a few, and liked their potential. In 1962, he decided to set out on his own, borrowing a lot of ideas for his early stores from Kmart and others. But it was what he chose to do differently—the ways he put his own stamp on the basic business model—that made Wal-Mart so fabulously successful. His model was the same as Kmart's, but his strategy was unique.

From the very start, for instance, Walton chose to serve a different group of customers in a different set of markets. The ten largest discounters in 1962, all gone today, focused on large metropolitan areas and cities like New York. Wal-Mart's "key strategy," in Walton's own words, "was to put good-sized stores into little one-horse towns which everybody else was ignoring."[3] He sought out isolated rural towns, like Rogers, with populations between 5,000 and 25,000. Being a small-town guy himself, Walton knew the terrain well. The nearest city was probably a four-hour drive away. He rightly bet that if his stores could match or beat the city prices, "people would shop at home." And since Wal-Mart's markets tended to be too small to support more than one large retailer, Walton was able to preempt competitors and discourage them from entering Wal-Mart's territory.

Wal-Mart also took a different approach to merchandising and pricing than its competitors did—that is, it promised customers a different kind of value. While competitors relied heavily on private label goods, second-tier brands, and price promotions, Wal-Mart promised national brands at everyday low prices. To make this promise more than a marketing slogan, the company pursued efficiency and reduced costs through innovative practices in areas such as purchasing, logistics, and information management.

The business model of discount retailing has attracted many players since it emerged in the 1950s. Most of them have failed. A few, like Wal-Mart and Target, have achieved superior performance over the long haul because their strategies set them apart. Wal-Mart offers branded goods for less to a carefully chosen customer base. Target built a strategy around a different kind of value—style and fashion. The losers in the industry—the chronic underperformers like Kmart—are companies that tried to be all things to all people. They failed to find distinctive ways to compete.

A Good Model Is Not Enough

There's another, more recent story that sheds further light on the relationship between business models and strategies. It's the story of Dell Computer. Unlike Sam Walton, Michael Dell was a true business-model pioneer. The model he created is, by now, well known: While other personal-computer makers sold through resellers, Dell sold directly to end customers. That not only cut out a costly link from the value chain, it also gave Dell the information it needed to manage inventory better than any other company in its industry. And because the pace of innovation in the industry was intense, Dell's inventory advantage meant it could avoid the high cost of obsolescence that other computer makers had to bear. Armed with its innovative business model, Dell has consistently outperformed rivals for more than a decade.

In this case, Dell's business model functioned much like a strategy: It made Dell different in ways that were hard to copy. If Dell's rivals tried to sell direct, they would disrupt their existing distribution channels and alienate the resellers on whom they relied. Trapped by their own strategies, they were damned if they copied Dell and damned if they didn't. When a new model changes the economics of an industry and is difficult to replicate, it can by itself create a strong competitive advantage.

What often gets lost in Dell's story, though, is the role that pure strategy has played in the company's superior performance. While Dell's direct business model laid out which value chain activities Dell would do (and which it wouldn't do), the company still had crucial strategic choices to make about which customers to serve and what kinds of products and services to offer. In the 1990s, for example, while other PC makers focused on computers for the home market, Dell consciously chose to go after large corporate accounts, which were far more profitable. Other PC makers offered low-end machines to lure in first-time buyers. Michael Dell wasn't interested in this "no-margin" business. He staked out his territory selling more powerful, higher margin computers.

Then, because Dell sold direct and could analyze its customers in depth, it began to notice that its average selling price to consumers was increasing while the industry's was falling. Consumers who were buying their second or third machines and who were looking for more power and less hand-holding were coming to Dell—even though it wasn't targeting them. Only in 1997, *after* it had a profitable, billion-dollar consumer business, did Dell dedicate a group to serving the consumer segment.

Now that everyone in its industry is selling direct, Dell's strategy has shifted to deal with the new competitive realities. With a decade-long lead, Dell is by far the industry's best executor of the direct-selling model—it is the low-cost producer. So it is using its cost advantage in PCs to compete on price, to gain share, and to drive the weaker players out of the business. At the same time, the company is relying on its core business model to pursue opportunities in new product markets, like servers, that have greater profit potential than PCs. The underlying business model remains the same. The strategic choices about where to apply the model—which geographic markets, which segments, which customers, which products—are what change.

Clarity about its business model has helped Dell in another way: as a basis for employee communication and motivation. Because a business model tells a good story, it can be used to get everyone in the organization aligned around the kind of value the company wants to create. Stories are easy to grasp and easy to remember. They help individuals to see their own jobs within the larger context of what the company is trying to do and to tailor their behavior accordingly. Used in this way, a good business model can become a powerful tool for improving execution.

Today, "business model" and "strategy" are among the most sloppily used terms in business; they are often stretched to mean everything—and end up meaning nothing. But as the experiences of companies like Dell and Wal-Mart show, these are concepts with enormous practical value. It's true that any attempt to draw sharp boundaries around abstract terms involves some arbitrary choices. But unless we're willing to draw the line somewhere, these concepts will remain confusing and difficult to use. Definition brings clarity. And when it comes to concepts that are so fundamental to performance, no organization can afford fuzzy thinking.

Notes

1. James C. Collins and Jerry I. Porras, *Built to Last* (Harper-Collins, 1994).
2. "Meg Whitman at eBay Inc. (A)," HBS case no.9-400-035.
3. "Wal-Mart Stores, Inc.," HBS case no. 9-794-024.

Originally published in May 2002
Reprint R0205F

Disruptive Technologies

Catching the Wave

JOSEPH L. BOWER AND
CLAYTON M. CHRISTENSEN

Executive Summary

ONE OF THE MOST CONSISTENT patterns in business is the failure of leading companies to stay at the top of their industries when technologies or markets change. Why is it that established companies invest aggressively—and successfully—in the technologies necessary to retain their current customers but then fail to make the technological investments that customers of the future will demand? The fundamental reason is that leading companies succumb to one of the most popular, and valuable, management dogmas: they stay close to their customers.

Customers wield extraordinary power in directing a company's investments. But what happens when a new technology emerges that customers reject because it *doesn't* address their needs as effectively as a company's current approach? In an ongoing study of technological change, the authors found that most established companies are consistently ahead of their industries in developing and commercializing new technologies as long as those technologies address the next-generation-performance needs of their customers. However, an industry's leaders are rarely in the forefront of commercializing new technologies that don't initially meet the functional demands of mainstream customers and appeal only to small or emerging markets.

To remain at the top of their industries, managers must first be able to spot the technologies that fall into this category. To pursue these technologies, managers must protect them from the processes and incentives that are geared to serving mainstream customers. And the only way to do that is to create organizations that are completely independent of the mainstream business.

ONE OF THE MOST CONSISTENT patterns in business is the failure of leading companies to stay at the top of their industries when technologies or markets change. Goodyear and Firestone entered the radial-tire market quite late. Xerox let Canon create the small-copier market. Bucyrus-Erie allowed Caterpillar and Deere to take over the mechanical excavator market. Sears gave way to Wal-Mart.

The pattern of failure has been especially striking in the computer industry. IBM dominated the mainframe market but missed by years the emergence of minicomputers, which were technologically much simpler than mainframes. Digital Equipment dominated the minicomputer market with innovations like its VAX architecture but missed the personal-computer market almost completely. Apple Computer led the world of personal computing and established the standard for user-friendly computing but lagged five years behind the leaders in bringing its portable computer to market.

Why is it that companies like these invest aggressively—and successfully—in the technologies necessary to retain their current customers but then fail to make certain other technological investments that customers of the future will demand? Undoubtedly, bureaucracy, arrogance, tired executive blood, poor planning, and short-term investment horizons have all played a role. But a more fundamental reason lies at the heart of the paradox: leading companies succumb to one of the most popular, and valuable, management dogmas. They stay close to their customers.

Although most managers like to think they are in control, customers wield extraordinary power in directing a company's investments. Before managers decide to launch a technology, develop a product, build a plant, or establish new channels of distribution, they must look to their customers first: Do their customers want it? How big will the market be? Will the investment be profitable? The more astutely managers ask and answer these questions, the more completely their investments will be aligned with the needs of their customers.

This is the way a well-managed company should operate. Right? But what happens when customers reject a new technology, product concept, or way of doing business because it does not address their needs as effectively as a company's current approach? The large photocopying centers that represented the core of Xerox's customer base at first had no use for small, slow tabletop copiers. The excavation contractors that had relied on Bucyrus-Erie's big-bucket steam- and diesel-powered cable shovels didn't want hydraulic excavators because initially they were small and weak. IBM's large commercial, government, and industrial customers saw no immediate use for minicomputers. In each instance, companies listened to their customers, gave them the product performance they were looking for, and, in the end, were hurt by the very technologies their customers led them to ignore.

We have seen this pattern repeatedly in an on-going study of leading companies in a variety of industries that have confronted technological change. The research shows that most well-managed, established companies are consistently ahead of their industries in developing and commercializing new technologies—from incremental improvements to radically new approaches—as long as those technologies address the next-generation performance needs of their customers. However, these same companies are rarely in the forefront of commercializing new technologies that don't initially meet the needs of mainstream customers and appeal only to small or emerging markets.

Using the rational, analytical investment processes that most well-managed companies have developed, it is nearly impossible to build a cogent case for diverting resources from known customer needs in established markets to markets and customers that seem insignificant or do not yet exist. After all, meeting the needs of established customers and fending off competitors takes all the resources a company has, and then some. In well-managed companies, the processes used to identify customers' needs, forecast technological trends, assess profitability, allocate resources across competing proposals for investment, and take new products to market are focused—for all the right reasons—on current customers and markets. These processes are designed to weed out proposed products and technologies that do *not* address customers' needs.

In fact, the processes and incentives that companies use to keep focused on their main customers work so well that they blind those companies to important new technologies in emerging markets. Many companies have learned the hard way the perils of ignoring new technologies that do not initially meet the needs of mainstream customers. For example, although personal computers did not meet the requirements of mainstream minicomputer users in the early 1980s, the computing power of the desktop machines improved at a much faster rate than minicomputer users' *demands* for computing power did. As a result, personal computers caught up with the computing needs of many of the customers of Wang, Prime, Nixdorf, Data General, and Digital Equipment. Today they are performance-competitive with minicomputers in many applications. For the minicomputer makers, keeping close to mainstream customers and ignoring what were initially low-performance desktop technologies used by seemingly insignificant customers in emerging markets was a rational decision—but one that proved disastrous.

The technological changes that damage established companies are usually not radically new or difficult from a *technological* point of view. They do, however, have two important characteristics: First, they typically present a different package of performance attributes—ones that, at least at the outset, are not valued by existing customers. Second, the performance attributes that existing customers do value improve at such a rapid rate that the new technology can later invade those established markets. Only at this point will mainstream customers want the technology. Unfortunately for the established suppliers, by then it is often too late: the pioneers of the new technology dominate the market.

It follows, then, that senior executives must first be able to spot the technologies that seem to fall into this category. Next, to commercialize and develop the new technologies, managers must protect them from the processes and incentives that are geared to serving established customers. And the only way to protect them is to create organizations that are completely independent from the mainstream business.

No industry demonstrates the danger of staying too close to customers more dramatically than the hard-disk-drive industry. Between 1976 and 1992, disk-drive performance improved at a stunning rate: the physical size of a 100-megabyte (MB) system shrank from 5,400 to 8 cubic inches, and the cost per MB fell from $560 to $5. Technological change, of course, drove these breathtaking achievements. About half of the improvement came from a host of radical advances that were critical to continued improvements in disk-drive performance; the other half came from incremental advances.

The pattern in the disk-drive industry has been repeated in many other industries: the leading, established companies have consistently led the industry in developing and adopting new technologies that their customers demanded—even when those technologies required completely different technological competencies and manufacturing capabilities from the ones the companies had. In spite of this aggressive technological posture, no single disk-drive manufacturer has been able to dominate the industry for more than a few years. A series of companies have entered the business and risen to prominence, only to be toppled by newcomers who pursued technologies that at first did not meet the needs of mainstream customers. As a result, not one of the independent disk-drive companies that existed in 1976 survives today.

To explain the differences in the impact of certain kinds of technological innovations on a given industry, the concept of *performance trajectories*—the rate at which the performance of a product has improved, and is expected to improve, over time—can be helpful. Almost every industry has a critical performance trajectory. In mechanical excavators, the critical trajectory is the annual improvement in cubic yards of earth moved per minute. In photocopiers, an important performance trajectory is improvement in number of copies per minute. In disk drives, one crucial measure of performance is storage capacity, which has advanced 50% each year on average for a given size of drive.

Different types of technological innovations affect performance trajectories in different ways. On the one hand, *sustaining* technologies tend to maintain a rate of improvement; that is, they give customers something more or better in the attributes they already value. For example, thin-film components in disk drives, which replaced conventional ferrite heads and oxide disks between 1982 and 1990, enabled information to be recorded more densely on disks. Engineers had been pushing the limits of the performance they could wring from ferrite heads and oxide disks, but the drives employing these technologies seemed to have reached the natural limits of an S curve. At that point, new thin film technologies emerged that restored—or sustained—the historical trajectory of performance improvement.

On the other hand, *disruptive* technologies introduce a very different package of attributes from the one mainstream customers historically value, and they often perform far worse along one or two dimensions that are particularly important to those customers. As a rule, mainstream customers are unwilling to use a disruptive product in applications they know and understand. At first, then, disruptive technologies tend to be used and valued only in new markets or new applications; in fact, they generally make possible the emergence of new markets. For example, Sony's early transistor radios sacrificed sound fidelity but created a market for portable radios by offering a new and different package of attributes—small size, light weight, and portability.

In the history of the hard-disk-drive industry, the leaders stumbled at each point of disruptive technological change: when the diameter of disk drives shrank from the original 14 inches to 8 inches, then to 5.25 inches, and finally to 3.5 inches. Each of these new architectures initially offered the market substantially less storage capacity than the typical user in the established market required. For example, the 8-inch drive offered 20 MB when it was introduced, while the primary market for disk drives at that time—mainframes—required 200 MB on average. Not surprisingly, the leading computer manufacturers rejected the 8-inch architecture at first. As a result, their suppliers, whose mainstream products consisted of 14-inch drives with more than 200 MB of capacity, did not pursue the disruptive products aggressively. The pattern was repeated when the 5.25-inch and 3.5-inch drives emerged: established computer makers rejected the drives as inadequate, and, in turn, their disk-drive suppliers ignored them as well.

But while they offered less storage capacity, the disruptive architectures created other important attributes—internal power supplies and smaller size (8-inch drives); still smaller size and low-cost stepper motors (5.25-inch drives); and ruggedness, light weight, and low power consumption (3.5-inch drives). From the late 1970s to the mid-1980s, the availability of the three drives made possible the development of new markets for minicomputers, desktop PCs, and portable computers, respectively.

Although the smaller drives represented disruptive technological change, each was technologically straight-forward. In fact, there were engineers at many leading companies who championed the new technologies and built working prototypes with bootlegged resources before management gave a formal go-ahead. Still, the leading companies could not move the products through their organizations and into the market in a timely way. Each time a disruptive technology emerged, between one-half and two-thirds of the established manufacturers failed to introduce models employing the new architecture—in stark contrast to their timely launches of critical sustaining technologies. Those companies that finally did launch new models typically lagged behind entrant companies by two years—eons in an industry whose products' life cycles are often two years. Three waves of entrant companies led these revolutions; they first captured the new markets and then dethroned the leading companies in the mainstream markets.

How could technologies that were initially inferior and useful only to new markets eventually threaten leading companies in established markets? Once the disruptive architectures became established in their new markets, sustaining innovations raised each architecture's performance along steep trajectories—so steep that the performance available from each architecture soon satisfied the needs of customers in the established markets. For example, the 5.25-inch drive, whose initial 5 MB of capacity in 1980 was only a fraction of the capacity that the minicomputer market needed, became fully performance-competitive in the minicomputer market by 1986 and in the mainframe market by 1991. (See the graph "How Disk-Drive Performance Met Market Needs.")

How Disk-Drive Performance Met Market Needs

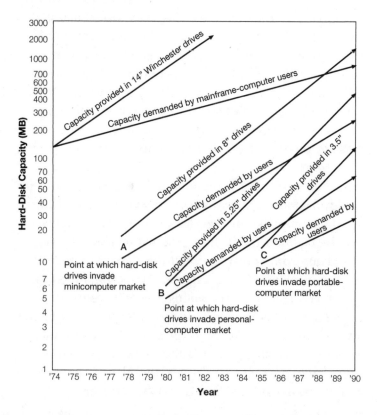

A company's revenue and cost structures play a critical role in the way it evaluates proposed technological innovations. Generally, disruptive technologies look financially unattractive to established companies. The potential revenues from the discernible markets are small, and it is often difficult to project how big the markets for the technology will be over the long term. As a result, managers typically conclude that the technology cannot make a meaningful contribution to corporate growth and, therefore, that it is not worth the management effort required to develop it. In addition, established companies have often installed higher cost structures to serve sustaining technologies than those required by disruptive technologies. As a result, managers typically see themselves as having two choices when deciding whether to pursue disruptive technologies. One is to go *downmarket* and accept the lower profit margins of the emerging markets that the disruptive technologies will initially serve. The other is to go *upmarket* with sustaining technologies and enter market segments whose profit margins are alluringly high. (For example, the margins of IBM's mainframes are still higher than those of PCs). Any rational resource-allocation process in companies serving established markets will choose going upmarket rather than going down.

Managers of companies that have championed disruptive technologies in emerging markets look at the world quite differently. Without the high cost structures of their established counterparts, these companies find the emerging markets appealing. Once the companies have secured a foothold in the markets and improved the performance of their technologies, the established markets above them, served by high-cost suppliers, look appetizing. When they do attack, the entrant companies find the established players to be easy and unprepared opponents because the opponents have been looking upmarket themselves, discounting the threat from below.

It is tempting to stop at this point and conclude that a valuable lesson has been learned: managers can avoid missing the next wave by paying careful attention to potentially disruptive technologies that do *not* meet current customers' needs. But recognizing the pattern and figuring out how to break it are two different things. Although entrants invaded established markets with new technologies three times in succession, none of the established leaders in the disk-drive industry seemed to learn from the experiences of those that fell before them. Management myopia or lack of foresight cannot explain these failures. The problem is that managers keep doing what has worked in the past: serving the rapidly growing needs of their current customers. The processes that successful, well-managed companies have developed to allocate resources among proposed investments are *incapable* of funneling resources into programs that current customers explicitly don't want and whose profit margins seem unattractive.

Managing the development of new technology is tightly linked to a company's investment processes. Most strategic proposals—to add capacity or to develop new products or processes—take shape at the lower levels of organizations in engineering groups or project teams. Companies then use analytical planning and budgeting systems to select from among the candidates competing for funds. Proposals to create new businesses in emerging markets are particularly challenging to assess because they depend on notoriously unreliable estimates of market size. Because managers are evaluated on their ability to place the right bets, it is not surprising that in well-managed companies, mid- and top-level managers back projects in which the market seems assured. By staying close to lead customers, as they have been trained to do, managers focus resources on fulfilling the requirements of those reliable customers that can be served profitably. Risk is reduced—and careers are safe-guarded—by giving known customers what they want.

Seagate Technology's experience illustrates the conse-quences of relying on such resource-allocation processes to evaluate disruptive technologies. By almost any mea-sure, Seagate, based in Scotts Valley, California, was one of the most successful and aggressively managed compa-nies in the history of the microelectronics industry: from its inception in 1980, Seagate's revenues had grown to more than $700 million by 1986. It had pioneered 5.25-inch hard-disk drives and was the main supplier of them to IBM and IBM-compatible personal-computer manufacturers. The company was the leading manufac-turer of 5.25-inch drives at the time the disruptive 3.5-inch drives emerged in the mid-1980s.

Engineers at Seagate were the second in the industry to develop working prototypes of 3.5-inch drives. By early 1985, they had made more than 80 such models with a low level of company funding. The engineers forwarded the new models to key marketing executives, and the trade press reported that Seagate was actively developing 3.5-inch drives. But Seagate's principal customers—IBM and other manufacturers of AT-class personal computers—showed no interest in the new drives. They wanted to incorporate 40-MB and 60-MB drives in their next-generation models, and Seagate's early 3.5-inch prototypes packed only 10 MB. In response, Seagate's marketing executives lowered their sales forecasts for the new disk drives.

Manufacturing and financial executives at the company pointed out another drawback to the 3.5-inch drives. According to their analysis, the new drives would never be competitive with the 5.25-inch architecture on a cost-per-megabyte basis—an important metric that Seagate's customers used to evaluate disk drives. Given Seagate's cost structure, margins on the higher-capacity 5.25-inch models therefore promised to be much higher than those on the smaller products.

Senior managers quite rationally decided that the 3.5-inch drive would not provide the sales volume and profit margins that Seagate needed from a new product. A former Seagate marketing executive recalled, "We needed a new model that could become the next ST412 [a 5.25-inch drive generating more than $300 million in annual sales, which was nearing the end of its life cycle]. At the time, the entire market for 3.5-inch drives was less than $50 million. The 3.5-inch drive just didn't fit the bill—for sales or profits."

The shelving of the 3.5-inch drive was *not* a signal that Seagate was complacent about innovation. Seagate subsequently introduced new models of 5.25-inch drives at an accelerated rate and, in so doing, introduced an impressive array of sustaining technological improvements, even though introducing them rendered a significant portion of its manufacturing capacity obsolete.

While Seagate's attention was glued to the personal-computer market, former employees of Seagate and other 5.25-inch drive makers, who had become frustrated by their employers' delays in launching 3.5-inch drives, founded a new company, Conner Peripherals. Conner focused on selling its 3.5-inch drives to companies in emerging markets for portable computers and small-footprint desktop products (PCs that take up a smaller amount of space on a desk). Conner's primary customer was Compaq Computer, a customer that Seagate had never served. Seagate's own prosperity, coupled with Conner's focus on customers who valued different disk-drive attributes (ruggedness, physical volume, and weight), minimized the threat Seagate saw in Conner and its 3.5-inch drives.

From its beachhead in the emerging market for portable computers, however, Conner improved the storage capacity of its drives by 50% per year. By the end of 1987, 3.5-inch drives packed the capacity demanded in the mainstream personal-computer market. At this point, Seagate executives took their company's 3.5-inch drive off the shelf, introducing it to the market as a *defensive* response to the attack of entrant companies like Conner and Quantum Corporation, the other pioneer of 3.5-inch drives. But it was too late.

By then, Seagate faced strong competition. For a while, the company was able to defend its existing market by selling 3.5-inch drives to its established customer base—manufacturers and resellers of full-size personal computers. In fact, a large proportion of its 3.5-inch products continued to be shipped in frames that enabled its customers to mount the drives in computers designed to accommodate 5.25-inch drives. But, in the end, Seagate could only struggle to become a second-tier supplier in the new portable-computer market.

In contrast, Conner and Quantum built a dominant position in the new portable-computer market and then used their scale and experience base in designing and manufacturing 3.5-inch products to drive Seagate from the personal-computer market. In their 1994 fiscal years, the combined revenues of Conner and Quantum exceeded $5 billion.

Seagate's poor timing typifies the responses of many established companies to the emergence of disruptive technologies. Seagate was willing to enter the market for 3.5-inch drives only when it had become large enough to satisfy the company's financial requirements—that is, only when existing customers wanted the new technology. Seagate has survived through its savvy acquisition of Control Data Corporation's disk-drive business in 1990. With CDC's technology base and Seagate's volume-manufacturing expertise, the company has become a powerful player in the business of supplying large-capacity drives for high-end computers. Nonetheless, Seagate has been reduced to a shadow of its former self in the personal-computer market.

It should come as no surprise that few companies, when confronted with disruptive technologies, have been able to overcome the handicaps of size or success. But it can be done. There is a method to spotting and cultivating disruptive technologies.

DETERMINE WHETHER THE TECHNOLOGY IS DISRUPTIVE OR SUSTAINING

The first step is to decide which of the myriad technologies on the horizon are disruptive and, of those, which are real threats. Most companies have well-conceived processes for identifying and tracking the progress of potentially sustaining technologies, because they are important to serving and protecting current customers. But few have systematic processes in place to identify and track potentially disruptive technologies.

One approach to identifying disruptive technologies is to examine internal disagreements over the development of new products or technologies. Who supports the project and who doesn't? Marketing and financial managers, because of their managerial and financial incentives, will rarely support a disruptive technology. On the other hand, technical personnel with outstanding track records will often persist in arguing that a new market for the technology will emerge—even in the face of opposition from key customers and marketing and financial staff. Disagreement between the two groups often signals a disruptive technology that top-level managers should explore.

DEFINE THE STRATEGIC SIGNIFICANCE OF THE DISRUPTIVE TECHNOLOGY

The next step is to ask the right people the right questions about the strategic importance of the disruptive technology. Disruptive technologies tend to stall early in strategic reviews because managers either ask the wrong questions or ask the wrong people the right questions. For example, established companies have regular procedures for asking mainstream customers—especially the important accounts where new ideas are actually tested—to assess the value of innovative products. Generally, these customers are selected because they are the ones striving the hardest to stay ahead of *their* competitors in pushing the performance of *their* products. Hence these customers are most likely to demand the highest performance from their suppliers. For this reason, lead customers are reliably accurate when it comes to assessing the potential of sustaining technologies, but they are reliably *in*accurate when it comes to assessing the potential of disruptive technologies. They are the wrong people to ask.

A simple graph plotting product performance as it is defined in mainstream markets on the vertical axis and time on the horizontal axis can help managers identify both the right questions and the right people to ask.

First, draw a line depicting the level of performance and the trajectory of performance improvement that customers have historically enjoyed and are likely to expect in the future. Then locate the estimated initial performance level of the new technology. If the technology is disruptive, the point will lie far below the performance demanded by current customers. (See the graph "How to Assess Disruptive Technologies.")

What is the likely slope of performance improvement of the disruptive technology compared with the slope of performance improvement demanded by existing markets? If knowledgeable technologists believe the new technology might progress faster than the market's demand for performance improvement, then that technology, which does not meet customers' needs today, may very well address them tomorrow. The new technology, therefore, is strategically critical.

How to Assess Disruptive Technologies

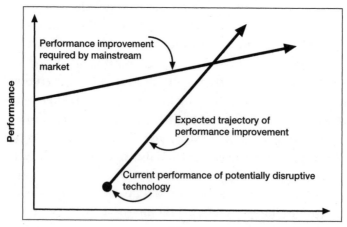

Performance improvement required by mainstream market

Expected trajectory of performance improvement

Current performance of potentially disruptive technology

Performance

Time

Instead of taking this approach, most managers ask the wrong questions. They compare the anticipated rate of performance improvement of the new technology with that of the established technology. If the new technology has the potential to surpass the established one, the reasoning goes, they should get busy developing it.

Pretty simple. But this sort of comparison, while valid for sustaining technologies, misses the central strategic issue in assessing potentially disruptive technologies. Many of the disruptive technologies we studied *never* surpassed the capability of the old technology. It is the trajectory of the disruptive technology compared with that of the *market* that is significant. For example, the reason the mainframe-computer market is shrinking is not that personal computers outperform mainframes but because personal computers networked with a file server meet the computing and data-storage needs of many organizations effectively. Mainframe-computer makers are reeling not because the performance of personal-computing technology surpassed the performance of mainframe *technology* but because it intersected with the performance demanded by the established *market*.

Consider the graph again. If technologists believe that the new technology will progress at the same rate as the market's demand for performance improvement, the disruptive technology may be slower to invade established markets. Recall that Seagate had targeted personal computing, where demand for hard-disk capacity per computer was growing at 30% per year. Because the capacity of 3.5-inch drives improved at a much faster rate, leading 3.5-inch-drive makers were able to force Seagate out of the market. However, two other 5.25-inch-drive makers, Maxtor and Micropolis, had targeted the engineering-workstation market, in which demand for hard-disk capacity was insatiable. In that market, the trajectory of capacity demanded was essentially parallel to the trajectory of capacity improvement that technologists could supply in the 3.5-inch architecture. As a result, entering the 3.5-inch-drive business was strategically less critical for those companies than it was for Seagate.

LOCATE THE INITIAL MARKET FOR THE DISRUPTIVE TECHNOLOGY

Once managers have determined that a new technology is disruptive and strategically critical, the next step is to locate the initial markets for that technology. Market research, the tool that managers have traditionally relied on, is seldom helpful: at the point a company needs to make a strategic commitment to a disruptive technology, no concrete market exists. When Edwin Land asked Polaroid's market researchers to assess the potential sales of his new camera, they concluded that Polaroid would sell a mere 100,000 cameras over the product's lifetime; few people they interviewed could imagine the uses of instant photography.

Because disruptive technologies frequently signal the emergence of new markets or market segments, managers must *create* information about such markets—who the customers will be, which dimensions of product performance will matter most to which customers, what the right price points will be. Managers can create this kind of information only by experimenting rapidly, iteratively, and inexpensively with both the product and the market.

For established companies to undertake such experiments is very difficult. The resource-allocation processes that are critical to profitability and competitiveness will not—and should not—direct resources to markets in which sales will be relatively small. How, then, can an established company probe a market for a disruptive technology? Let start-ups—either ones the company funds or others with no connection to the company— conduct the experiments. Small, hungry organizations are good at placing economical bets, rolling with the punches, and agilely changing product and market strategies in response to feedback from initial forays into the market.

Consider Apple Computer in its start-up days. The company's original product, the Apple I, was a flop when it was launched in 1977. But Apple had not placed a huge bet on the product and had gotten at least *something* into the hands of early users quickly. The company learned a lot from the Apple I about the new technology and about what customers wanted and did not want. Just as important, a group of customers learned about what they did and did not want from personal computers. Armed with this information, Apple launched the Apple II quite successfully.

Many companies could have learned the same valuable lessons by watching Apple closely. In fact, some companies pursue an explicit strategy of being *second to invent*—allowing small pioneers to lead the way into uncharted market territory. For instance, IBM let Apple, Commodore, and Tandy define the personal computer. It then aggressively entered the market and built a considerable personal-computer business.

But IBM's relative success in entering a new market late is the exception, not the rule. All too often, successful companies hold the performance of small-market pioneers to the financial standards they apply to their own performance. In an attempt to ensure that they are using their resources well, companies explicitly or implicitly set relatively high thresholds for the size of the markets they should consider entering. This approach sentences them to making late entries into markets already filled with powerful players.

For example, when the 3.5-inch drive emerged, Seagate needed a $300-million-a-year product to replace its mature flagship 5.25-inch model, the ST412, and the 3.5-inch market wasn't large enough. Over the next two years, when the trade press asked when Seagate would introduce its 3.5-inch drive, company executives consistently responded that there was no market yet. There actually *was* a market, and it was growing rapidly. The signals that Seagate was picking up about the market, influenced as they were by customers who didn't want 3.5-inch drives, were misleading. When Seagate finally introduced its 3.5-inch drive in 1987, more than $750 million in 3.5-inch drives had already been sold. Information about the market's size had been widely available throughout the industry. But it wasn't compelling enough to shift the focus of Seagate's managers. They continued to look at the new market through the eyes of their current customers and in the context of their current financial structure.

The posture of today's leading disk-drive makers toward the newest disruptive technology, 1.8-inch drives, is eerily familiar. Each of the industry leaders has designed one or more models of the tiny drives, and the models are sitting on shelves. Their capacity is too low to be used in notebook computers, and no one yet knows where the initial market for 1.8-inch drives will be. Fax machines, printers, and automobile dashboard mapping systems are all candidates. "There just isn't a market," complained one industry executive. "We've got the product, and the sales force can take orders for it. But there are no orders because nobody needs it. It just sits there." This executive has not considered the fact that his sales force has no incentive to sell the 1.8-inch drives instead of the higher-margin products it sells to higher-volume customers. And while the 1.8-inch drive is sitting on the shelf at his company and others, last year more than $50 million worth of 1.8-inch drives were sold, almost all by start-ups. This year, the market will be an estimated $150 million.

To avoid allowing small, pioneering companies to dominate new markets, executives must personally monitor the available intelligence on the progress of pioneering companies through monthly meetings with technologists, academics, venture capitalists, and other nontraditional sources of information. They *cannot* rely on the company's traditional channels for gauging markets because those channels were not designed for that purpose.

PLACE RESPONSIBILITY FOR BUILDING A DISRUPTIVE-TECHNOLOGY BUSINESS IN AN INDEPENDENT ORGANIZATION

The strategy of forming small teams into skunk-works projects to isolate them from the stifling demands of mainstream organizations is widely known but poorly understood. For example, isolating a team of engineers so that it can develop a radically new sustaining technology just because that technology is radically different is a fundamental misapplication of the skunk-works approach. Managing out of context is also unnecessary in the unusual event that a disruptive technology is more financially attractive than existing products. Consider

Intel's transition from dynamic random access memory (DRAM) chips to microprocessors. Intel's early microprocessor business had a higher gross margin than that of its DRAM business; in other words, Intel's normal resource-allocation process naturally provided the new business with the resources it needed.[1]

Creating a separate organization is necessary only when the disruptive technology has a lower profit margin than the mainstream business and must serve the unique needs of a new set of customers. CDC, for example, successfully created a remote organization to commercialize its 5.25-inch drive. Through 1980, CDC was the dominant independent disk-drive supplier due to its expertise in making 14-inch drives for mainframe-computer makers. When the 8-inch drive emerged, CDC launched a late development effort, but its engineers were repeatedly pulled off the project to solve problems for the more profitable, higher-priority 14-inch projects targeted at the company's most important customers. As a result, CDC was three years late in launching its first 8-inch product and never captured more than 5% of that market.

When the 5.25-inch generation arrived, CDC decided that it would face the new challenge more strategically. The company assigned a small group of engineers and marketers in Oklahoma City, Oklahoma, far from the mainstream organization's customers, the task of developing and commercializing a competitive 5.25-inch product. "We needed to launch it in an environment in which everybody got excited about a $50,000 order," one executive recalled. "In Minneapolis, you needed a $1 million order to turn anyone's head." CDC never regained the 70% share it had once enjoyed in the market for mainframe disk drives, but its Oklahoma City operation secured a profitable 20% of the high-performance 5.25-inch market.

Had Apple created a similar organization to develop its Newton personal digital assistant (PDA), those who have pronounced it a flop might have deemed it a success. In launching the product, Apple made the mistake of acting as if it were dealing with an established market. Apple managers went into the PDA project assuming that it had to make a significant contribution to corporate growth. Accordingly, they researched customer desires exhaustively and then bet huge sums launching the Newton. Had Apple made a more modest technological and financial bet and entrusted the Newton to an organization the size that Apple itself was when it launched the Apple I, the outcome might have been different. The Newton might have been seen more broadly as a solid step forward in the quest to discover what customers really want. In fact, many more Newtons than Apple I models were sold within a year of their introduction.

KEEP THE DISRUPTIVE ORGANIZATION INDEPENDENT

Established companies can only dominate emerging markets by creating small organizations of the sort CDC created in Oklahoma City. But what should they do when the emerging market becomes large and established?

Most managers assume that once a spin-off has become commercially viable in a new market, it should be integrated into the mainstream organization. They reason that the fixed costs associated with engineering, manufacturing, sales, and distribution activities can be shared across a broader group of customers and products.

This approach might work with sustaining technologies; however, with disruptive technologies, folding the spin-off into the mainstream organization can be disastrous. When the independent and mainstream organizations are folded together in order to share resources, debilitating arguments inevitably arise over which groups get what resources and whether or when to cannibalize established products. In the history of the disk-drive industry, *every* company that has tried to manage mainstream and disruptive businesses within a single organization failed.

No matter the industry, a corporation consists of business units with finite life spans: the technological and market bases of any business will eventually disappear. Disruptive technologies are part of that cycle. Companies that understand this process can create new businesses to replace the ones that must inevitably die. To do so, companies must give managers of disruptive innovation free rein to realize the technology's full potential—even if it means ultimately killing the mainstream business. For the corporation to live, it must be willing to see business units die. If the corporation doesn't kill them off itself, competitors will.

The key to prospering at points of disruptive change is not simply to take more risks, invest for the long term, or fight bureaucracy. The key is to manage strategically important disruptive technologies in an organizational context where small orders create energy, where fast low-cost forays into ill-defined markets are possible, and where overhead is low enough to permit profit even in emerging markets.

Managers of established companies can master disruptive technologies with extraordinary success. But when they seek to develop and launch a disruptive technology that is rejected by important customers within the context of the mainstream business's financial demands, they fail—not because they make the wrong decisions, but because they make the right decisions for circumstances that are about to become history.

Notes

1. Robert A. Burgelman, "Fading Memories: A Process Theory of Strategic Business Exit in Dynamic Environments," *Administrative Science Quarterly* 39 (1994), pp. 24–56.

Originally published January–February 1995
Reprint 3510

Reinventing Your Business Model

MARK W. JOHNSON, CLAYTON M.
CHRISTENSEN, AND HENNING KAGERMANN

Executive Summary

WHY IS IT SO DIFFICULT for established companies to pull off the new growth that business model innovation can bring? Here's why: They don't understand their current business model well enough to know if it would suit a new opportunity or hinder it, and they don't know how to build a new model when they need it.

Drawing on their vast knowledge of disruptive innovation and experience in helping established companies capture game-changing opportunities, consultant Johnson, Harvard Business School professor Christensen, and SAP co-CEO Kagermann set out the tools that executives need to do both.

Successful companies already operate according to a business model that can be broken down into four elements: a *customer value proposition* that fulfills an important job for the customer in a better way than competitors' offerings do; a *profit formula* that lays out how the company makes money delivering the value proposition; and the *key resources* and *key processes* needed to deliver that proposition.

Game-changing opportunities deliver radically new customer value propositions: They fulfill a job to be done in a dramatically better way (as P&G did with its Swiffer mops), solve a problem that's never been solved before (as Apple did with its iPod and iTunes electronic entertainment delivery system), or serve an entirely unaddressed customer base (as Tata Motors is doing with its Nano—the $2,500 car aimed at Indian families who use scooters to get around). Capitalizing on such opportunities doesn't always require a new business model: P&G, for instance, didn't need a new one to leverage its product innovation strengths to develop the Swiffer.

A new model is often needed, however, to leverage a new technology (as in Apple's case); is generally required when the opportunity addresses an entirely new group of customers (as with the Nano); and is surely in order when an established company needs to fend off a successful disruptor (as the Nano's competitors may now need to do).

In 2003, APPLE introduced the iPod with the iTunes store, revolutionizing portable entertainment, creating a new market, and transforming the company. In just three years, the iPod/iTunes combination became a nearly $10 billion product, accounting for almost 50% of Apple's revenue. Apple's market capitalization catapulted from around $1 billion in early 2003 to over $150 billion by late 2007.

This success story is well known; what's less well known is that Apple was not the first to bring digital music players to market. A company called Diamond Multimedia introduced the Rio in 1998. Another firm, Best Data, introduced the Cabo 64 in 2000. Both products worked well and were portable and stylish. So why did the iPod, rather than the Rio or Cabo, succeed?

Apple did something far smarter than take a good technology and wrap it in a snazzy design. It took a good technology and wrapped it in a great business model. Apple's true innovation was to make downloading digital music easy and convenient. To do that, the company built a groundbreaking business model that combined hardware, software, and service. This approach worked like Gillette's famous blades-and-razor model in reverse: Apple essentially gave away the "blades" (low-margin iTunes music) to lock in purchase of the "razor" (the high-margin iPod). That model defined value in a new way and provided game-changing convenience to the consumer.

Business model innovations have reshaped entire industries and redistributed billions of dollars of value. Retail discounters such as Wal-Mart and Target, which entered the market with pioneering business models, now account for 75% of the total valuation of the retail sector. Low-cost U.S. airlines grew from a blip on the radar screen to 55% of the market value of all carriers. Fully 11 of the 27 companies born in the last quarter century that grew their way into the *Fortune* 500 in the past 10 years did so through business model innovation.

Stories of business model innovation from well-established companies like Apple, however, are rare. An analysis of major innovations within existing corporations in the past decade shows that precious few have been business-model related. And a recent American Management Association study determined that no more than 10% of innovation investment at global companies is focused on developing new business models.

Yet everyone's talking about it. A 2005 survey by the Economist Intelligence Unit reported that over 50% of executives believe business model innovation will become even more important for success than product or service innovation. A 2008 IBM survey of corporate CEOs echoed these results. Nearly all of the CEOs polled reported the need to adapt their business models; more than two-thirds said that extensive changes were required. And in these tough economic times, some CEOs are already looking to business model innovation to address permanent shifts in their market landscapes.

Senior managers at incumbent companies thus confront a frustrating question: Why is it so difficult to pull off the new growth that business model innovation can bring? Our research suggests two problems. The first is a lack of definition: Very little formal study has been done into the dynamics and processes of business model development. Second, few companies understand their existing business model well enough—the premise behind its development, its natural interdependencies, and its strengths and limitations. So they don't know when they can leverage their core business and when success requires a new business model.

After tackling these problems with dozens of companies, we have found that new business models often look unattractive to internal and external stakeholders—at the outset. To see past the borders of what is and into the land of the new, companies need a road map.

Ours consists of three simple steps. The first is to realize that success starts by not thinking about business models at all. It starts with thinking about the opportunity to satisfy a real customer who needs a job done. The second step is to construct a blueprint laying out how your company will fulfill that need at a profit. In our model, that plan has four elements. The third is to compare that model to your existing model to see how much you'd have to change it to capture the opportunity. Once you do, you will know if you can use your existing model and organization or need to separate out a new unit to execute a new model. Every successful company is already fulfilling a real customer need with an effective business model, whether that model is explicitly understood or not. Let's take a look at what that entails.

Business Model: A Definition

A business model, from our point of view, consists of four interlocking elements that, taken together, create and deliver value. The most important to get right, by far, is the first.

CUSTOMER VALUE PROPOSITION (CVP)

A successful company is one that has found a way to create value for customers—that is, a way to help customers get an important job done. By "job" we mean a fundamental problem in a given situation that needs a solution. Once we understand the job and all its dimensions, including the full process for how to get it done, we can design the offering. The more important the job is to the customer, the lower the level of customer satisfaction with current options for getting the job done, and the better your solution is than existing alternatives at getting the job done (and, of course, the lower the price), the greater the CVP. Opportunities for creating a CVP are at their most potent, we have found, when alternative products and services have not been designed with the real job in mind and you can design an offering that gets that job—and only that job—done perfectly. We'll come back to that point later.

PROFIT FORMULA

The profit formula is the blueprint that defines how the company creates value for itself while providing value to the customer. It consists of the following:

- *Revenue model:* price × volume

- *Cost structure:* direct costs, indirect costs, economies of scale. Cost structure will be predominantly driven by the cost of the key resources required by the business model.

- *Margin model:* given the expected volume and cost structure, the contribution needed from each transaction to achieve desired profits.

- *Resource velocity:* how fast we need to turn over inventory, fixed assets, and other assets—and, overall, how well we need to utilize resources—to support our expected volume and achieve our anticipated profits.

People often think the terms "profit formulas" and "business models" are interchangeable. But how you make a profit is only one piece of the model. We've found it most useful to start by setting the price required to deliver the CVP and then work backwards from there to determine what the variable costs and gross margins must be. This then determines what the scale and resource velocity needs to be to achieve the desired profits.

KEY RESOURCES

The key resources are assets such as the people, technology, products, facilities, equipment, channels, and brand required to deliver the value proposition to the targeted customer. The focus here is on the *key* elements that create value for the customer and the company, and the way those elements interact. (Every company also has generic resources that do not create competitive differentiation.)

KEY PROCESSES

Successful companies have operational and managerial processes that allow them to deliver value in a way they can successfully repeat and increase in scale. These may include such recurrent tasks as training, development, manufacturing, budgeting, planning, sales, and service. Key processes also include a company's rules, metrics, and norms.

These four elements form the building blocks of any business. The customer value proposition and the profit formula define value for the customer and the company, respectively; key resources and key processes describe how that value will be delivered to both the customer and the company.

As simple as this framework may seem, its power lies in the complex interdependencies of its parts. Major changes to any of these four elements affect the others and the whole. Successful businesses devise a more or less stable system in which these elements bond to one another in consistent and complementary ways.

How Great Models Are Built

To illustrate the elements of our business model framework, we will look at what's behind two companies' game-changing business model innovations.

CREATING A CUSTOMER VALUE PROPOSITION

It's not possible to invent or reinvent a business model without first identifying a clear customer value proposition. Often, it starts as a quite simple realization. Imagine, for a moment, that you are standing on a Mumbai road on a rainy day. You notice the large number of motor scooters snaking precariously in and out around the cars. As you look more closely, you see that most bear whole families—both parents and several children. Your first thought might be "That's crazy!" or "That's the way it is in developing countries—people get by as best they can."

When Ratan Tata of Tata Group looked out over this scene, he saw a critical job to be done: providing a safer alternative for scooter families. He understood that the cheapest car available in India cost easily five times what a scooter did and that many of these families could not afford one. Offering an affordable, safer, all-weather alternative for scooter families was a powerful value proposition, one with the potential to reach tens of millions of people who were not yet part of the car-buying market. Ratan Tata also recognized that Tata Motors' business model could not be used to develop such a product at the needed price point.

The Elements of a Successful Business Model

Every successful company already operates according to an effective business model. By systematically identifying all of its constituent parts, executives can understand how the model fulfills a potent value proposition in a profitable way using certain key resources and key processes. With that understanding, they can then judge how well the same model could be used to fulfill a radically different CVP—and what they'd need to do to construct a new one, if need be, to capitalize on that opportunity.

Customer Value Proposition (CVP)
- **Target customer**
- **Job to be done** to solve an important problem or fulfill an important need for the target customer
- **Offering,** which satisfies the problem or fulfills the need. This is defined not only by what is sold but also by how it's sold.

Profit Formula
- **Revenue model:** How much money can be made: price x volume. Volume can be thought of in terms of market size, purchase frequency, ancillary sales, etc.
- **Cost structure:** How costs are allocated: includes cost of key assets, direct costs, indirect costs, economies of scale.
- **Margin model:** How much each transaction should net to achieve desired profit levels.
- **Resource velocity:** How quickly resources need to be used to support target volume. Includes lead times, throughput, inventory turns, asset utilization, and so on.

Key Resources needed to deliver the customer value proposition profitably. Might include:
- **People**
- **Technology, products**
- **Equipment**
- **Information**
- **Channels**
- **Partnerships, alliances**
- **Brand**

Key Processes, as well as rules, metrics, and norms, that make the profitable delivery of the customer value proposition repeatable and scalable. Might include:
- **Processes:** design, product development, sourcing, manufacturing, marketing, hiring and training, IT
- **Rules and metrics:** margin requirements for investment, credit terms, lead times, supplier terms
- **Norms:** opportunity size needed for investment, approach to customers and channels

At the other end of the market spectrum, Hilti, a
Liechtenstein-based manufacturer of high-end power tools
for the construction industry, reconsidered the real job to
be done for many of its current customers. A contractor
makes money by finishing projects; if the required tools
aren't available and functioning properly, the job doesn't
get done. Contractors don't make money by *owning* tools;
they make it by using them as efficiently as possible. Hilti
could help contractors get the job done by selling tool *use*
instead of the tools themselves—managing its customers'
tool inventory by providing the best tool at the right time
and quickly furnishing tool repairs, replacements, and
upgrades, all for a monthly fee. To deliver on that value
proposition, the company needed to create a fleet-
management program for tools and in the process shift

Hilti Sidesteps Commoditization

*Hilti is capitalizing on a game-changing opportunity to increase
profitability by turning products into a service. Rather than sell
tools (at lower and lower prices), it's selling a "just-the-tool-you-
need-when-you-need-it, no-repair-or-storage-hassles" service.
Such a radical change in customer value proposition required
a shift in all parts of its business model.*

Traditional Power Tool Company		Hilti's Tool Fleet Management Service
Sales of industrial and professional power tools and accessories	Customer value proposition	Leasing a comprehensive fleet of tools to increase contractors' on-site productivity
Low margins, high inventory turnover	Profit formula	Higher margins; asset heavy; monthly payments for tool maintenance, repair, and replacement
Distribution channel, low-cost manufacturing plants in developing countries, R&D	Key resources and processes	Strong direct-sales approach, contract management, IT systems for inventory management and repair, warehousing

its focus from manufacturing and distribution to service. That meant Hilti had to construct a new profit formula and develop new resources and new processes.

The most important attribute of a customer value proposition is its precision: how perfectly it nails the customer job to be done—and nothing else. But such precision is often the most difficult thing to achieve. Companies trying to create the new often neglect to focus on *one* job; they dilute their efforts by attempting to do lots of things. In doing lots of things, they do nothing *really* well.

One way to generate a precise customer value proposition is to think about the four most common barriers keeping people from getting particular jobs done: insufficient wealth, access, skill, or time. Software maker Intuit devised QuickBooks to fulfill small-business owners' need to avoid running out of cash. By fulfilling that job with greatly simplified accounting software, Intuit broke the *skills barrier* that kept untrained small-business owners from using more-complicated accounting packages. MinuteClinic, the drugstore-based basic health care provider, broke the *time barrier* that kept people from visiting a doctor's office with minor health issues by making nurse practitioners available without appointments.

DESIGNING A PROFIT FORMULA

Ratan Tata knew the only way to get families off their scooters and into cars would be to break the *wealth barrier* by drastically decreasing the price of the car. "What if I can change the game and make a car for one lakh?" Tata wondered, envisioning a price point of around US$2,500, less than half the price of the cheapest car available. This, of course, had dramatic ramifications for the profit formula: It required both a significant drop in gross margins and a radical reduction in many elements of the cost structure. He knew, however, he could still make money if he could increase sales volume dramatically, and he knew that his target base of consumers was potentially huge.

For Hilti, moving to a contract management program required shifting assets from customers' balance sheets to its own and generating revenue through a lease/ subscription model. For a monthly fee, customers could have a full complement of tools at their fingertips, with repair and maintenance included. This would require a fundamental shift in all major components of the profit formula: the revenue stream (pricing, the staging of payments, and how to think about volume), the cost structure (including added sales development and contract management costs), and the supporting margins and transaction velocity.

IDENTIFYING KEY RESOURCES AND PROCESSES

Having articulated the value proposition for both the customer and the business, companies must then consider the key resources and processes needed to deliver that value. For a professional services firm, for example, the key resources are generally its people, and the key processes are naturally people related (training and development, for instance). For a packaged goods company, strong brands and well-selected channel retailers might be the key resources, and associated brand-building and channel-management processes among the critical processes.

Oftentimes, it's not the individual resources and processes that make the difference but their relationship to one another. Companies will almost always need to integrate their key resources and processes in a unique way to get a job done perfectly for a set of customers. When they do, they almost always create enduring competitive advantage. Focusing first on the value proposition and the profit formula makes clear how those resources and processes need to interrelate. For example, most general hospitals offer a value proposition that might be described as, "We'll do anything for anybody." Being all things to all people requires these hospitals to have a vast collection of resources (specialists, equipment, and so on) that can't be knit together in any proprietary way. The result is not just a lack of differentiation but dissatisfaction.

By contrast, a hospital that focuses on a specific value proposition can integrate its resources and processes in a unique way that delights customers. National Jewish Health in Denver, for example, is organized around a focused value proposition we'd characterize as, "If you have a disease of the pulmonary system, bring it here. We'll define its root cause and prescribe an effective therapy." Narrowing its focus has allowed National Jewish to develop processes that integrate the ways in which its specialists and specialized equipment work together.

For Tata Motors to fulfill the requirements of its customer value proposition and profit formula for the Nano, it had to reconceive how a car is designed, manufactured, and distributed. Tata built a small team of fairly young engineers who would not, like the company's more-experienced designers, be influenced and constrained in their thinking by the automaker's existing profit formulas. This team dramatically minimized the number of parts in the vehicle, resulting in a significant cost saving. Tata also reconceived its supplier strategy, choosing to outsource a remarkable 85% of the Nano's components and use nearly 60% fewer vendors than normal to reduce transaction costs and achieve better economies of scale.

At the other end of the manufacturing line, Tata is envisioning an entirely new way of assembling and distributing its cars. The ultimate plan is to ship the modular components of the vehicles to a combined network of company-owned and independent entrepreneur-owned assembly plants, which will build them to order. The Nano will be designed, built, distributed, and serviced in a radically new way—one that could not be accomplished without a new business model. And while the jury is still out, Ratan Tata may solve a traffic safety problem in the process.

For Hilti, the greatest challenge lay in training its sales representatives to do a thoroughly new task. Fleet management is not a half-hour sale; it takes days, weeks, even months of meetings to persuade customers to buy a program instead of a product. Suddenly, field reps accustomed to dealing with crew leaders and on-site purchasing managers in mobile trailers found themselves staring down CEOs and CFOs across conference tables.

Additionally, leasing required new resources— new people, more robust IT systems, and other new technologies—to design and develop the appropriate packages and then come to an agreement on monthly payments. Hilti needed a process for maintaining large arsenals of tools more inexpensively and effectively than its customers had. This required warehousing, an inventory management system, and a supply of replacement tools. On the customer management side, Hilti developed a website that enabled construction managers to view all the tools in their fleet and their usage rates. With that information readily available, the managers could easily handle the cost accounting associated with those assets.

Rules, norms, and metrics are often the last element to emerge in a developing business model. They may not be fully envisioned until the new product or service has been road tested. Nor should they be. Business models need to have the flexibility to change in their early years.

When a New Business Model Is Needed

Established companies should not undertake business-model innovation lightly. They can often create new products that disrupt competitors without fundamentally changing their own business model. Procter & Gamble, for example, developed a number of what it calls "disruptive market innovations" with such products as the Swiffer disposable mop and duster and Febreze, a new kind of air freshener. Both innovations built on P&G's existing business model and its established dominance in household consumables.

There are clearly times, however, when creating new growth requires venturing not only into unknown market territory but also into unknown business model territory. When? The short answer is "When significant changes are needed to all four elements of your existing model." But it's not always that simple. Management judgment is clearly required. That said, we have observed five strategic circumstances that often require business model change:

1. The opportunity to address through disruptive innovation the needs of large groups of potential customers who are shut out of a market entirely because existing solutions are too expensive or complicated for them. This includes the opportunity to democratize products in emerging markets (or reach the bottom of the pyramid), as Tata's Nano does.

2. The opportunity to capitalize on a brand-new technology by wrapping a new business model around it (Apple and MP3 players) or the opportunity to leverage a tested technology by bringing it to a whole new market (say, by offering military technologies in the commercial space or vice versa).

3. The opportunity to bring a job-to-be-done focus where one does not yet exist. That's common in industries where companies focus on products or customer segments, which leads them to refine existing products more and more, increasing commoditization over time. A jobs focus allows companies to redefine industry profitability. For example, when FedEx entered the package delivery market, it did not try to compete through lower prices or better marketing. Instead, it concentrated on fulfilling an entirely unmet customer need to receive packages far, far faster, and more reliably, than any service then could. To do so, it had to integrate its key processes and resources in a vastly more efficient way. The business model that resulted from this job-to-be-done emphasis gave FedEx a significant competitive advantage that took UPS many years to copy.

4. The need to fend off low-end disrupters. If the Nano is successful, it will threaten other automobile makers, much as minimills threatened the integrated steel mills a generation ago by making steel at significantly lower cost.

5. The need to respond to a shifting basis of competition. Inevitably, what defines an acceptable solution in a market will change over time, leading core market segments to commoditize. Hilti needed to change its

business model in part because of lower global manufacturing costs; "good enough" low-end entrants had begun chipping away at the market for high-quality power tools.

Of course, companies should not pursue business model reinvention unless they are confident that the opportunity is large enough to warrant the effort. And, there's really no point in instituting a new business model unless it's not only new to the company but in some way new or game-changing to the industry or market. To do otherwise would be a waste of time and money.

These questions will help you evaluate whether the challenge of business model innovation will yield acceptable results. Answering "yes" to all four greatly increases the odds of successful execution:

- Can you nail the job with a focused, compelling customer value proposition?

- Can you devise a model in which all the elements— the customer value proposition, the profit formula, the key resources, and the key processes—work together to get the job done in the most efficient way possible?

- Can you create a new business development process unfettered by the often negative influences of your core business?

- Will the new business model disrupt competitors?

Creating a new model for a new business does not mean the current model is threatened or should be changed. A new model often reinforces and complements the core business, as Dow Corning discovered.

How Dow Corning Got Out of Its Own Way

When business model innovation is clearly called for, success lies not only in getting the model right but also in making sure the incumbent business doesn't in some way prevent the new model from creating value or thriving. That was a problem for Dow Corning when it built a new business unit—with a new profit formula—from scratch.

For many years, Dow Corning had sold thousands of silicone-based products and provided sophisticated technical services to an array of industries. After years of profitable growth, however, a number of product areas were stagnating. A strategic review uncovered a critical insight: Its low-end product segment was commoditizing. Many customers experienced in silicone application

Dow Corning Embraces the Low End

Traditionally high-margin Dow Corning found new opportunities in low-margin offerings by setting up a separate business unit that operates in an entirely different way. By fundamentally differentiating its low-end and high-end offerings, the company avoided cannibalizing its traditional business even as it found new profits at the low end.

Established Business		New Business Unit
Customized solutions, negotiated contracts	**Customer value proposition**	No frills, bulk prices, sold through the internet
High-margin, high-overhead retail prices pay for value-added services	**Profit formula**	Spot-market pricing, low overhead to accommodate lower margins, high throughput
R&D, sales, and service orientation	**Key resources and processes**	IT system, lowest-cost processes, maximum automation

no longer needed technical services; they needed basic products at low prices. This shift created an opportunity for growth, but to exploit that opportunity Dow Corning had to figure out a way to serve these customers with a lower-priced product. The problem was that both the business model and the culture were built on high-priced, innovative product and service packages. In 2002, in pursuit of what was essentially a commodity business for low-end customers, Dow Corning CEO Gary Anderson asked executive Don Sheets to form a team to start a new business.

The team began by formulating a customer value proposition that it believed would fulfill the job to be done for these price-driven customers. It determined that the price point had to drop 15% (which for a commoditizing material was a huge reduction). As the team analyzed what that new customer value proposition would require, it realized reaching that point was going to take a lot more than merely eliminating services. Dramatic price reduction would call for a different profit formula with a fundamentally lower cost structure, which depended heavily on developing a new IT system. To sell more products faster, the company would need to use the internet to automate processes and reduce overhead as much as possible.

BREAKING THE RULES

As a mature and successful company, Dow Corning was full of highly trained employees used to delivering its high-touch, customized value proposition. To automate, the new business would have to be far more standardized, which meant instituting different and, overall, much stricter rules. For example, order sizes would be limited to a few, larger-volume options; order lead times would fall between two and four weeks (exceptions would cost extra);

and credit terms would be fixed. There would be charges if a purchaser required customer service. The writing was on the wall: The new venture would be low- touch, self-service, and standardized. To succeed, Dow Corning would have to break the rules that had previously guided its success.

Sheets next had to determine whether this new venture, with its new rules, could succeed within the confines of Dow Corning's core enterprise. He set up an experimental war game to test how existing staff and systems would react to the requirements of the new customer value proposition. He got crushed as entrenched habits and existing processes thwarted any attempt to change the game. It became clear that the corporate antibodies would kill the initiative before it got off the ground. The way forward was clear: The new venture had to be free from existing rules and free to decide what rules would be appropriate in order for the new commodity line of business to thrive. To nurture the opportunity—and also protect the existing model—a new business unit with a new brand identity was needed. Xiameter was born.

IDENTIFYING NEW COMPETENCIES

Following the articulation of the new customer value proposition and new profit formula, the Xiameter team focused on the new competencies it would need, its key resources and processes. Information technology, just a small part of Dow Corning's core competencies at that time, emerged as an essential part of the now web-enabled business. Xiameter also needed employees who could make smart decisions very quickly and who would thrive in a fast-changing environment, filled initially with lots of ambiguity. Clearly, new abilities would have to be brought into the business.

Although Xiameter would be established and run as a separate business unit, Don Sheets and the Xiameter team did not want to give up the incumbency advantage that deep knowledge of the industry and of their own products gave them. The challenge was to tap into the expertise without importing the old-rules mind-set. Sheets conducted a focused HR search within Dow Corning for risk takers. During the interview process, when he came across candidates with the right skills, he asked them to take the job on the spot, before they left the room. This approach allowed him to cherry-pick those who could make snap decisions and take big risks.

THE SECRET SAUCE: PATIENCE

Successful new businesses typically revise their business models four times or so on the road to profitability. While a well-considered business-model-innovation process can often shorten this cycle, successful incumbents must tolerate initial failure and grasp the need for course correction. In effect, companies have to focus on learning and adjusting as much as on executing. We recommend companies with new business models be patient for growth (to allow the market opportunity to unfold) but impatient for profit (as an early validation that the model works). A profitable business is the best early indication of a viable model.

Accordingly, to allow for the trial and error that naturally accompanies the creation of the new while also constructing a development cycle that would produce results and demonstrate feasibility with minimal resource outlay, Dow Corning kept the scale of Xiameter's operation small but developed an aggressive timetable for launch and set the goal of becoming profitable by the end of year one.

Xiameter paid back Dow Corning's investment in just three months and went on to become a major, transformative success. Beforehand, Dow Corning had had no online sales component; now 30% of sales originate online, nearly three times the industry average. Most of these customers are new to the company. Far from cannibalizing existing customers, Xiameter has actually supported the main business, allowing Dow Corning's sales-people to more easily enforce premium pricing for their core offerings while providing a viable alternative for the price-conscious.

Established companies' attempts at transformative growth typically spring from product or technology innovations. Their efforts are often characterized by prolonged development cycles and fitful attempts to find a market. As the Apple iPod story that opened this article suggests, truly transformative businesses are never exclusively about the discovery and commercialization of a great technology. Their success comes from enveloping the new technology in an appropriate, powerful business model.

Bob Higgins, the founder and general partner of Highland Capital Partners, has seen his share of venture success and failure in his 20 years in the industry. He sums up the importance and power of business model innovation this way: "I think historically where we [venture capitalists] fail is when we back technology. Where we succeed is when we back new business models."

When the Old Model Will Work

YOU DON'T ALWAYS NEED a new business model to capitalize on a game-changing opportunity. Sometimes, as P&G did with its Swiffer, a company finds that its current model is revolutionary in a new market. When will the old model do? When you can fulfill the new customer value proposition:

- With your current profit formula
- Using most, if not all, of your current key resources and processes
- Using the same core metrics, rules, and norms you now use to run your business

What Rules, Norms, and Metrics Are Standing in Your Way?

IN ANY BUSINESS, a fundamental understanding of the core model often fades into the mists of institutional memory, but it lives on in rules, norms, and metrics put in place to protect the status quo (for example, "Gross margins must be at 40%"). They are the first line of defense against any new model's taking root in an existing enterprise.

Financial
- Gross margins
- Opportunity size

- Unit pricing
- Unit margin
- Time to breakeven
- Net present value calculations
- Fixed cost investment
- Credit items

Operational

- End-product quality
- Supplier quality
- Owned versus outsourced manufacturing
- Customer service
- Channels
- Lead times
- Throughput

Other

- Pricing
- Performance demands
- Product-development life cycles
- Basis for individuals' rewards and incentives
- Brand parameters

Originally published in December 2008
Reprint R0812C

Building Breakthrough Businesses Within Established Organizations

VIJAY GOVINDARAJAN AND CHRIS TRIMBLE

Executive Summary

MANY COMPANIES assume that once they've launched a major innovation, growth will soon follow. It's not that simple. High-potential new businesses within established companies face stiff headwinds well after their inception. That's why a company's emphasis must shift: from ideas to execution and from leadership excellence to organizational excellence.

The authors spent five years chronicling new businesses at the New York Times Company, Analog Devices, Corning, Hasbro, and other organizations. They found that a breakthrough new business (referred to as NewCo) rarely coexists gracefully with the established business in the company (called CoreCo). The unnatural combination creates three specific challenges—*forgetting, borrowing,* and *learning*—that NewCo must meet in order to survive and grow.

NewCo must first forget some of what made CoreCo successful. NewCo and CoreCo have elemental differences, so NewCo must leave behind CoreCo's notions about what skills and competencies are most valuable.

NewCo must also borrow some of CoreCo's assets—usually in one or two key areas that will give NewCo a crucial competitive advantage. Incremental cost reductions, for example, are never a sufficient justification for borrowing.

Finally, NewCo must be prepared to learn some things from scratch. Because strategic experiments are highly uncertain endeavors, NewCo will face several critical unknowns. The more rapidly it can resolve those unknowns—that is, the faster it can learn—the sooner it will zero in on a winning business model or exit a hopeless situation. Managers can accelerate this learning by planning more simply and more often and by comparing predicted and actual trends.

FEW BUSINESS NARRATIVES are more evocative than that of the inspired leader boldly pursuing an extraordinarily innovative idea. So romantic is the notion that companies pushing for more innovation often devote the bulk of their energies and resources to generating ideas and encouraging individual initiatives. This is a good start, but nothing more. New businesses with the potential to deliver breakthrough growth for established companies face stiff headwinds well after launch. Ray Stata, a cofounder of Analog Devices, the $2 billion semiconductor company, has lived this challenge for decades: "I came to the conclusion long ago that limits to innovation have less to do with technology or creativity than organizational agility. Inspired individuals can only do so much." Emphasis must shift: from ideas to execution and from leadership excellence to organizational excellence.

To find out exactly what it takes to get beyond ideas, we have spent the past five years chronicling initiatives at organizations such as the New York Times Company, Analog Devices, Corning, Hasbro, Cisco, Unilever, Kodak, Johnson & Johnson, Nucor, Stora Enso, and the Thomson Corporation. We have examined best practices for managing strategic experiments—high-growth-potential new businesses that depart from an organization's current business model and that target emerging industries in which no clear formula exists for making a profit. Strategic experiments constitute the highest-risk, highest-return category of innovation and require a unique managerial approach. We chose to focus on strategic experiments because dramatic forces such as globalization, digital technology, biotechnology, and demographic change are now creating nonlinear shifts in the economy—threatening stability but also opening up opportunities for breakthrough growth.

A new business with high growth potential (let's call it NewCo) rarely coexists gracefully with the most closely related established business unit within the company (let's call it CoreCo). The unnatural combination creates three specific challenges for NewCo: *forgetting, borrowing,* and *learning.* NewCo must forget some of what made CoreCo successful, because NewCo and CoreCo have elemental differences. NewCo must borrow some of CoreCo's assets—the greatest advantage it has over independent start-ups. And NewCo must be prepared to learn some things from scratch.

When Analog Devices decided to explore opportunities presented by a new semiconductor technology, it faced all three challenges. The technology, called microelectromechanical systems (MEMS), uses a chip with microscopic moving parts that act as sensors; the first commercial application was automotive crash sensors, which launch airbags. The MEMS team at Analog Devices needed to *forget*, because the company's core business model wouldn't work for MEMS. Analog Devices was accustomed to serving thousands of customers with thousands of products, many designed for custom applications. There were only a few automakers, however, and because they valued cost and reliability over customization, they needed only a few variations on the basic crash sensor. As a result, the MEMS team had to alter all of its processes for selling, marketing, and manufacturing. The team also needed to *borrow* Analog Devices' semiconductor expertise and manufacturing plants. And it needed to *learn* whether MEMS devices could be manufactured at a profit and to what extent markets for MEMS applications outside the automotive industry would develop. The business ultimately became profitable but not without first having to confront each of the three challenges.

Forgetting, borrowing, and learning are monumental tasks. That's why it's crucial for a company to leverage the power of organizational design—a term we use in its broadest sense. In building NewCo, the CEO must be willing to challenge the status quo on an extraordinary range of issues: hiring, individual performance evaluation, needed competencies, reporting relationships, decision rights, planning and budgeting, business performance assessment, metrics, compensation, shared values, and shared assumptions about success.

The three challenges are present throughout NewCo's awkward adolescence, from launch to profitability. And they're present all at once, which means tackling them requires an understanding of how they're related. Forgetting and borrowing are at odds, for example, and need to be balanced. A sole focus on forgetting would suggest isolation of NewCo, while a sole focus on borrowing would suggest full integration of NewCo. Also, failure to forget cripples the learning effort. If NewCo cannot leave behind CoreCo's formula for success, it will not find its own.

Forget

To build a foundation for success, NewCo must forget CoreCo's business model. NewCo's answers to the fundamental questions that define a business—Who is our customer? What value do we offer? How do we deliver that value?—should be different from CoreCo's. NewCo must therefore leave behind notions about what skills and competencies are most valuable. And it must forget the relative predictability of CoreCo's environment.

It is easy to underestimate the magnitude of the forgetting challenge. And it is easy to conclude too quickly that NewCo has succeeded in forgetting. Awareness of the differences between NewCo and CoreCo is not enough. Forgetting is about changing behavior. Often, we have observed, NewCo talks like NewCo but acts like CoreCo.

Many powerful sources of institutional memory—instincts developed through past experiences, relationships between employees that are grounded in CoreCo's business model, performance measures, planning templates, norms for individual performance evaluation, and even often-told stories about the company's history—can interfere with forgetting. Some companies have especially strong memories. (See the insert "Warning Signs That

Forgetting Will Be an Uphill Battle" at the end of this article.)

Many firms make the mistake of duplicating CoreCo's organizational design when they create NewCo. Doing so minimizes hassles, since making NewCo an exception to rules about such things as hiring, compensation, and status can lead to resistance, even resentment, within CoreCo. But the only way to erase memory is to overhaul NewCo's organizational design.

To understand what it takes to forget, consider Corning's venture into the genomics industry. Through the 1990s, advances in biotechnology spawned an industry dedicated to serving the needs of genomics researchers, who were trying to unlock the secrets of DNA and unleash a revolution in medical therapies. Millions of new experiments became possible, and researchers desperately wanted to automate and accelerate the experimentation process.

One crucial piece of laboratory apparatus was the DNA microarray—a glass slide with thousands of tiny DNA samples adhered to it. Because of issues of quality, reliability, and ease of use, many researchers "printed" their own microarrays—a time-consuming and costly process. The opportunity for Corning was clear: to leverage its world-class expertise in specialty glass and microscopic manufacturing processes so it could offer genomics researchers a reliable and inexpensive supply of microarrays. When Corning launched Corning Microarray Technologies (CMT) in 1998, analysts were projecting explosive growth for the industry.

Over the years, Corning had been effective in part because its business units shared a common formula for success. Each sold components to industrial manufacturers. Each emphasized high quality and reliability. Each depended on strong intellectual property rights that limited competition. Each relied on excellence in the manufacture of glass and ceramics and on mastery of related scientific fields. Each planned in a disciplined fashion, and each held managers accountable to those plans.

But CMT was different. CMT sold to an unfamiliar customer—senior laboratory administrators. It needed to emphasize cost and convenience instead of the highest possible quality. It had to work in an unfamiliar, emerging scientific field where patent protection was unlikely. It needed to balance expertise in glass manufacturing with expertise in molecular biology. And it faced a much higher level of ambiguity.

The differences between Corning and CMT are clear in hindsight. But at the time, Corning naturally assumed that what had worked for its established business units would also work for CMT. Therefore, CMT had its own manufacturing, sales, and marketing functions and shared Corning's centralized research and development functions. CMT also adopted Corning's rigorous five-stage model for new product development, along with clear expectations for hitting certain milestones. Because CMT was small, it reported to the existing life sciences business unit. Corning did depart from its tradition of hiring and promoting from within—CMT hired several outside experts in molecular biology, many of whom were assigned to the centralized R&D groups—but all management positions were filled by Corning insiders. As a result, CMT did not develop a culture or identity that was noticeably different from Corning's.

Nonetheless, within months, CMT achieved its first success. It offered researchers who printed their own microarrays a much-improved *un*printed glass slide (without DNA adhered to it) with a special coating.

Customers were thrilled with the improved consistency they achieved in printing their own microarrays.

Ambitions for CMT escalated. Its leaders thought that if they simply stuck to the plan, breakthrough growth and profitability would certainly follow. But CMT soon faced unanticipated difficulties.

Working with DNA presented unfamiliar challenges. DNA from different suppliers had chemical inconsistencies, and Corning's usual methods for identifying and correcting manufacturing problems were confounded by the peculiarities of DNA fluid. One day the process would appear to be working fine; the next day a mysterious new problem would arise.

Soon CMT started missing deadlines established in the business plan. The leadership team felt intense pressure. Corning held managers accountable to the plan. Falling short was failing. Plus, falling behind meant that CMT would drag down the profitability of Corning's life sciences unit, which was just as concerned about hitting its numbers. Rather than reexamine fundamental choices, which would have meant admitting failure and asking for more capital, CMT leaders viewed their struggles as minor setbacks, and they urged their team to work harder.

Despite the high level of urgency, CMT was unable to meet expectations. In an environment of perceived failure, the cohesiveness of the leadership group frayed. The team often settled disagreements by reverting to what had worked in the past. Antagonism also developed between the molecular biology experts that CMT had hired from outside Corning and the CMT leadership team. The molecular biologists took issue with the way the leadership team allocated resources and evaluated outcomes. The biologists also disagreed with decisions to delay product launches to achieve quality standards they knew to be unnecessary in the imperfect world of biotechnology.

All of CMT's struggles stemmed from failures to forget. And all were probably inevitable from the moment CMT adopted Corning's organizational design.

Two years into CMT's operations, turnover in Corning's senior staff led to a reevaluation. Corning's leaders decided to rebuild the CMT organization. First, they appointed a new general manager, someone who had the ability to manage in ambiguous contexts and had a knack for facilitating communication between businesspeople, engineers, and scientists. Second, they reduced the extent to which CMT was integrated with the existing research and development functions by having CMT's heads of R&D report to CMT's general manager. Third, they changed to more subjective criteria for evaluating the general manager's performance, focusing on factors such as how quickly he learned and made adjustments. Fourth, the general manager no longer reported to the head of the life sciences business but to the president of Corning Technologies, who would dedicate significant time and energy to advising CMT.

CMT's new general manager subsequently made his own changes. He hired an outside molecular biology expert to manage the product development effort and another to manage relationships with suppliers. He also moved numerous CMT employees working in distant Corning facilities back to Corning, New York, to help CMT develop a distinct culture.

All of these changes took several months, but it was time well spent. CMT was able to restructure its relationships between research, development, marketing, and sales and to follow a more iterative innovation process. The molecular biologists were given a stronger voice and were able to help CMT make more rapid technical progress. And Corning's senior management team treated CMT's projections as though they were informed estimates rather than a nonnegotiable basis for judging performance. Knowing that he would be evaluated on how quickly he learned and made adjustments, CMT's general manager frequently updated the president on setbacks, lessons, and new directions. When CMT launched its first microarray product in September 2000, customers rated the product a "home run."

How to Forget

From studying Corning's experience—and comparing it to similar efforts at other companies—we have isolated a number of best practices for forgetting.

DON'T BE INSULAR

NewCo should hire outsiders in key management roles and strongly consider an outsider to head the business. Outsiders challenge institutional memory and are instrumental in building new competencies.

DON'T ASSIGN STATUS BASED ON SIZE

NewCo should report at least one level above CoreCo in order to reduce the pressures on NewCo for short-term results and to ensure that CoreCo does not hoard resources.

REARRANGE THE MOVING PARTS

NewCo should reconsider how major business functions such as marketing and product development interact.

Established patterns of interaction within CoreCo are usually incompatible with the new business model.

BUILD A NEW DASHBOARD

The company should not base NewCo's performance on CoreCo's metrics. Doing so reinforces CoreCo's formula for success, not NewCo's.

DARE TO MAKE COMPLEX JUDGMENTS

The company should not judge the performance of NewCo's leader too heavily against plans.

PROMOTE NEW THINKING ABOUT SUCCESS

NewCo's leader should create a unique set of beliefs about actions that lead to success and regularly reinforce them. CoreCo's beliefs may not apply in NewCo's environment.

Borrow

NewCo forgets most easily if it is isolated from CoreCo. But complete separation is impractical. CoreCo's tremendous resources are too valuable to ignore.

NewCo *could* borrow a lot from CoreCo—everything from unique assets such as a brand, a network of sales relationships, and manufacturing capacity, to more routine items such as hiring policies, accounting systems, and purchasing processes. We suggest a more measured approach. Borrow too much, and it becomes too hard to forget.

NewCo should borrow when it can gain a crucial competitive advantage—crucial enough that the company would highlight it in a pitch to outside investors. Corning, for example, could not credibly talk to shareholders about its investment in CMT without directing attention to its existing expertise in glass manufacturing. That's a sign that Corning's expertise in glass manufacturing is something CMT should borrow. Usually, there are only one or two such areas that meet this criteria. Incremental cost reductions are never sufficient justification for borrowing.

Links between NewCo and CoreCo should be selected carefully because if NewCo has been properly designed to forget, interactions will be difficult to manage. In fact, once the links are in place, the crux of the borrowing challenge then becomes anticipating the tensions between NewCo and CoreCo—and never allowing them to escalate beyond productive levels. Managing these interactions deserves substantial attention from senior management. Otherwise, cooperation between NewCo and CoreCo can easily disintegrate.

The story of the New York Times Company's venture into the interactive world demonstrates the difficulties of borrowing. The company launched its Internet business unit, eventually named New York Times Digital (NYTD), in 1995. At first, Internet operations were kept closely integrated with newspaper operations. The Internet team prepared content by altering headlines, adding hyperlinks, resizing photos, changing captions, and so forth, keeping the Web site up-to-date throughout the night until the final edition went to press. NYTD added many new features in the early years, but it soon started lagging behind competitors, which were more fully utilizing the rapidly expanding capability of the Internet. Though the NYTD staff pushed to keep pace, it felt constrained to a simple "newspaper.com" operation.

Soon, the company decided on a complete organizational overhaul, choosing an approach similar to Corning's.

The head of NYTD began reporting directly to the president rather than to the general manager of the *Times*. NYTD's managers created their own policy team, including a CFO and heads of human resources and business development. They hired so many outsiders with Internet experience that, by the end of 2000, only one-fourth of the staff had come through internal transfers. They altered planning norms and focused on different measures of performance. They moved to a separate building. And they made an effort to redefine their culture and values.

An explosion of creativity followed. The NYTD employees were now operating under the assumption that they served a different set of readers and advertisers than the *Times* and met distinct needs. They experimented with potential revenue sources and added a great deal of content that was not in the daily newspaper, including material from other news sources, audio and video content, interactive features, continuous news breaks, and *Times* archives.

Unfortunately, the organizational overhaul that enabled NYTD to forget also hindered its borrowing. Tensions heightened in the daily interactions between NYTD and the *Times*. And borrowing was absolutely crucial. NYTD needed two links in particular to the *Times*. Most obvious, NYTD could not survive without the newspaper's branded content, the main attraction for its readers. And NYTD needed to tap into the newspaper's existing base of advertisers, which required the coordination of sales processes.

Some tensions arose from substantive business conflicts. For example, the *Times* circulation department, quite understandably, was not enamored with NYTD. Making newspaper content available on the Internet at no charge gave people a powerful reason not to subscribe to the print version of the newspaper. Also, the *Times* editorial staff was concerned about protecting the newspaper's brand. NYTD was primarily a software operation and, as such, was designed to encourage cross-functional collaboration, something strictly limited within the newspaper to ensure that journalism was not influenced by commercial pressures. Finally, the *Times* group that sold display advertisements (as opposed to classifieds) viewed coordination with the NYTD sales team as a distraction, since the *Times* print ads were much bigger sources of revenue.

Tensions rooted in rivalry were also disruptive. NYTD received a great deal of media attention, especially when the company proposed, though never launched, a NYTD tracking stock that would have given NYTD employees a chance at a large payoff. And because NYTD had made it so clear that it was trying to build a different kind of organization, interactions took on an "us versus them" undertone. NYTD communicated that it aimed to be fast moving, antibureaucratic, risk taking, and experimental. Naturally, the *Times* aspired to be the same and winced at the implication that it was not.

These tensions are hardly unique. They are an inevitable part of the challenge of managing strategic experiments. We observed similar tensions in every company we studied. (For more on these tensions, see the insert "Warning Signs That Borrowing Will Be an Uphill Battle" at the end of this article.)

Whereas other companies in our research struggled to create effective cooperation, the New York Times Company succeeded because the senior management team acknowledged and proactively managed the tensions. The president, in particular, closely monitored interactions between NYTD and the *Times* and intervened when necessary to keep interactions productive.

In addition, in performance reviews of individual managers, the company stressed collaborating across business units. And to minimize tensions over subscription cannibalization, the senior management team conducted an analysis showing that cannibalization was minimal and that the Web site was actually generating new subscriptions by inducing trial use of the product online.

In most cases, the company empowered NYTD in its interactions with the *Times*. For example, to help NYTD establish a clear price in the market, the senior management team prohibited any initiative on the part of the *Times* to give away Web advertising as part of a larger print advertising package. (Editorial was one area where the company didn't empower NYTD. To protect the *Times* brand, the newspaper retained substantial control over alterations to editorial content on the Web site.)

NYTD reached profitability in 2001, in part because company leaders carefully managed interactions between NYTD and the *Times*. By 2004, NYTD was earning more than $30 million annually on revenues of approximately $100 million.

How to Borrow

Ultimately, NewCo has a much better chance of success when it can leverage CoreCo's assets. The trick, however, is borrowing only where the leverage is highest and ensuring that the senior management team is engaged in monitoring and facilitating. By comparing the New York Times' approach to those of other companies we studied, we were able to identify a number of best practices for borrowing.

BALANCE THE YIN OF FORGETTING WITH THE YANG OF BORROWING

Create links, yes, but only to lend NewCo a crucial competitive advantage. Avoid links where conflicts are severe. Avoid links to the IT or HR departments.

FIND COMMON GROUND

Reinforce values that NewCo and CoreCo share. In most cases, CoreCo will have some values that are inconsistent with NewCo's business model. Still, the senior management team can facilitate cooperation by creating a "metaculture" composed of more general values.

BE CAREFUL WHAT YOU ASK FOR

To promote collaboration, reconsider individual incentives. Evaluate and reward CoreCo managers, in part, according to their willingness to cooperate with NewCo. Avoid strong incentives tied strictly to CoreCo's short-term performance.

CO-OPT CORECO

To eliminate resistance from CoreCo's general manager, make borrowing as painless as possible so that he can focus strictly on CoreCo. Replenish CoreCo's resources when NewCo borrows heavily. Set transfer prices high enough to ensure that CoreCo will consider it a priority to help NewCo but not so high that NewCo cannot realistically achieve profitability. NewCo's profitability is a powerful symbol. CoreCo will always be more enthusiastic about helping when there is evidence that NewCo is succeeding.

BE ALERT TO TREMORS

Assign a senior executive to anticipate tensions between NewCo and CoreCo and to intervene should those tensions become destructive. The senior executive must be willing to commit a lot of time and energy and must be influential and respected within the corporation. She must continually explain the rationale for the differences between NewCo and CoreCo.

FORCE AUTHORITY UPHILL

Unless NewCo is in danger of damaging one of CoreCo's assets, particularly a brand, empower NewCo in its interactions with CoreCo. Without intervention, power will naturally shift back to the larger, more entrenched CoreCo.

Learn

Strategic experiments are highly uncertain endeavors. Regardless of the level of prior research and analysis, NewCo will face several critical unknowns. The faster it can resolve these unknowns—that is, the faster it learns— the sooner it will zero in on a winning business model or exit a hopeless situation.

Any new business has a great deal to learn—new skills to hone, new processes to perfect, new relationships to master. These are important. But the fundamental uncertainties in the business model itself will make or break the business. NewCo's leaders can resolve the critical unknowns most quickly by focusing on a specific task: learning to predict NewCo's business outcomes. At the outset, predictions are always wild guesses. It is not uncommon for revenue forecasts for three years out to be off by a factor of ten. But as the management team learns, wild guesses become informed estimates, and informed estimates become reliable forecasts. (See the exhibit "Is NewCo Learning?")

Because predictions are bound to be wrong, especially early on, it is tempting to put little effort into them or quickly discard them. This is a trap. You cannot get better at making predictions by avoiding them. Predictions are important not because of their accuracy but because of the learning opportunities they present. In fact, the crucial learning step for NewCo is analyzing disparities between predictions and outcomes. This analysis must be open and candid. And it must be conducted with speed, rigor, and discipline.

The learning challenge is the most difficult of the three. (See the insert "Warning Signs That Learning Will Be an

---

Is NewCo Learning?

Reliable forecasts are the best indicators that a new business is learning.

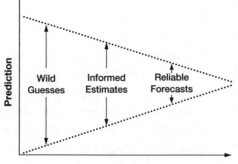

Uphill Battle" at the end of this article.) In fact, none of the companies we studied implemented a robust learning process that led to the quick resolution of critical unknowns. Thus, in our field research, we learned much more about what can go wrong than what can go right. The story of Hasbro Interactive illustrates several of the possible pitfalls associated with learning.

In 1995, Hasbro's traditional game business, with iconic brands such as Scrabble and Monopoly, was under threat. The ubiquitous PC, with its rapidly expanding multimedia capabilities, appeared to be the future of gaming. Viewing the threat as an opportunity, Hasbro created Hasbro Interactive. With a distinct organizational design and limited links to the core business, Hasbro Interactive succeeded both in forgetting and borrowing. But it would soon struggle with learning.

Hasbro Interactive's initial strategy was conservative. Executives there focused on converting existing Hasbro products to an interactive format. The new products were a quick success, generating $80 million in revenues and earning a profit in 1997. Hasbro touted Hasbro Interactive's potential to Wall Street analysts.

The division planned to double revenues in 1998. But to get there, Hasbro Interactive would have to pursue much more experimental possibilities. At this point, learning became even more important. Starting in early 1998, Hasbro Interactive bought licenses to produce games based on television shows. They purchased old video game properties, hoping to resurrect classics from the 1980s. They created deals with sports franchises. They acquired other video game producers. They expanded the video game platforms to serve more than just PCs. They began developing their own titles from scratch. And they invested heavily in a new Internet platform, Games.com.

Overall, the heightened ambition was consistent with the anything-is-possible atmosphere of the late 1990s. But the way that Hasbro Interactive pursued growth brought a tremendous number of additional unknowns into the business. For example, did Hasbro Interactive have the skills to develop products from scratch? Could it turn other companies' products into video games as successfully as its own? How quickly would video game players migrate to the Internet? Hasbro Interactive needed an effective learning process to quickly resolve these and other unknowns. Instead, it kept moving ahead aggressively for as long as possible.

Results were strong once again in 1998. Consequently, even though many of the new initiatives had yet to prove themselves, Hasbro Interactive set an audacious target: $1 billion in revenues within three years. The goal was initially just conversational, but it affected decision making and fueled ambition.

Nobody could know it at the time, but as the goal of reaching $1 billion coalesced, Hasbro Interactive entered a new period in its history—the beginning of the end. Results in the first quarter of 1999 were disappointing because of unexpectedly high returns of unsold product from retailers after the 1998 Christmas season. Senior executives at Hasbro became more alert. They had many questions. Concerns heightened when Hasbro Interactive reported a significant loss at the end of 1999—in the tens of millions of dollars. The pressure was on, and it only got worse when Hasbro's core business suffered a slight decline in 2000.

Hasbro Interactive was unable to quickly restore profitability. It had invested a great deal in experimental opportunities and did not want to abandon them before they had a realistic chance to succeed. The end came late in 2000, when turnover in Hasbro's senior management team led to a change in sentiment. The new team would not endure additional losses, and Hasbro Interactive was sold at a disappointing price.

Had Hasbro Interactive been engaged in a learning process from the beginning, a more favorable outcome would have been likely. The business would have been able to part with the specific initiatives that were failing, and it could have continued to build on those that were succeeding. But Hasbro Interactive did not learn quickly because its predictions were not treated with care. They were ignored, they were manipulated, and they became too rigid.

For a variety of reasons, Hasbro Interactive *ignored* its own predictions. First, it dismissed the importance of making them, believing they would be wrong anyway. Its executives felt they were in an all-out race for first-mover advantage and should be focused on doing, not planning. Second, like most companies, Hasbro's planning cycle was annual. But the planning cycle is also the learning cycle. Thus, Hasbro Interactive ignored the fundamental assumptions underlying predictions throughout the year, and learning slowed to a crawl. A quarterly or even monthly frequency would have been a better match for Hasbro Interactive's fast-changing business.

Managers of Hasbro's established toy and game business *manipulated* Hasbro Interactive's predictions by imposing their own performance measures. Starting in 1999, Hasbro held monthly meetings to review the performance of all Hasbro business units. Naturally, the instinct was to evaluate Hasbro Interactive just like any other Hasbro division. For example, Hasbro placed heavy emphasis on short-term profitability—an unrealistic measure, given Hasbro Interactive's risky initiatives. And when Hasbro

Interactive's returns from the retail trade were excessive by toy and game standards, it looked bad—even though the terms of trade are very different in software. Finally, when Hasbro Interactive argued that its product development expenses could be capitalized rather than expensed, a practice common in the software industry, others became uncomfortable because the practice was unfamiliar in toys and games. Thus, the measures that shaped the perceived performance of Hasbro Interactive were not those that could help resolve critical unknowns.

Hasbro Interactive also made the mistake of letting its predictions become *too rigid*. For years, Hasbro had applied relatively forgiving standards of accountability to plans because of the inherent unpredictability of the toy business. At the prodding of a senior executive hired from the outside, however, Hasbro had stiffened its standards, which made it unlikely that predictions for Hasbro Interactive could be revised.

Leaders of potentially high-growth businesses often view themselves as bold visionaries, and this also can interfere with the necessary revision of predictions. When it became clear that 1999 revenues would fall short, Hasbro Interactive's leader reaffirmed his belief in the original plan. He insisted on staying the course and continued to promote the $1 billion goal.

CEOs can also inadvertently make predictions inflexible. They may speak loudly of a new business's potential—as Hasbro's top executives did—both to insiders and outsiders. The intent may be to get investors excited, or it may be to increase CoreCo's support for NewCo. But doing so can lock in an overly aggressive prediction. The voice of the CEO is extremely powerful, and expectations can stick.

Rigid predictions, especially long-term ones, often lead to "guardrail-to-guardrail" decision making—that is, aggressive investment followed by complete abandonment. Such a pattern is the opposite of the gradual zeroing-in pattern that marks a healthy learning process. Hasbro Interactive went guardrail to guardrail in large part because of its heavy focus on the $1 billion revenue goal. Tensions escalated as time went by, and people's ability to rationally assess the situation became almost impossible. In the end, those who never believed that $1 billion was feasible managed to drown out the voices of those who saw the potential in Hasbro Interactive—and Hasbro Interactive was abandoned altogether.

How to Learn

Learning is the most difficult of the three challenges. It requires stepping away from tried-and-true, disciplined, and rigorous approaches to planning and moving to something very different but just as disciplined and rigorous. To promote effective learning.

DON'T TRY TO MIX OIL AND WATER

Hold separate meetings for evaluating the business performance of NewCo and CoreCo. These meetings must be handled very differently, and combining them can be impractical, if not destructive.

PROTECT PREDICTIONS

Ensure that executives involved in NewCo's planning process understand the importance of improving predictions and are aware of how this learning process can go astray when predictions are ignored, are manipulated, or become rigid.

AVOID BEING DEFENSIVE

Evaluate the leader of NewCo not on results but on his ability to learn and make good decisions. Though accountability to plans is an effective practice in mature businesses, it can be crippling in new high-potential businesses. If NewCo's leader is held accountable to the business plan, he will become defensive once targets are missed—a highly likely outcome in any strategic experiment. He will have a hard time being open and candid and may even hide information, perhaps even taking the senior management team out of the learning process altogether.

DO LESS, FASTER

That is, simplify plans, but plan more often. Each cycle through the planning process creates a learning opportunity, so planning more frequently increases the learning rate. To make a higher frequency practical, plans must be simplified. Detailed plans (broken down by region, product line, sales channel, and so forth) are useful for mature businesses, but NewCo should focus on resolving critical unknowns, which can be accomplished at a more aggregate level.

ANALYZE THROUGH A NEW LENS

Compare predicted and actual *trends*. Because strategic experiments are dynamic, rates of change are often more valuable information than current results.

MEASURE WHAT YOU DON'T KNOW

Identify metrics that are most useful in resolving critical unknowns. These are usually nonfinancial measures and are rarely the most closely watched metrics at CoreCo.

Opportunities to lead strategic experiments do not come along every day. In fact, we have encountered very few managers who have led such experiments more than once. Strategic experiments are adventures, and they are challenging—perhaps the "triple flip with a quadruple twist" of general management.

Thus, it is imperative that companies try to learn from others' experiences. The central lesson of history is this: To convert breakthrough ideas into breakthrough growth, you must forget, borrow, and learn. Each has straightforward principles.

Today's executives celebrate an innovation myth focused on gifted visionaries. But the capabilities of the organizations that surround these visionaries will make or break the visions.

Warning Signs That Forgetting Will Be an Uphill Battle

- The company has only one business model.
- All business units within the company are at similar points in the business life cycle (starting up, rapidly growing, steadily expanding, maturing, or declining).
- CoreCo has well-established standards of business performance that do not apply to NewCo—often because NewCo has a different cost structure.

- The company has a well-defined culture and has effective socialization mechanisms built into its hiring and acquisition processes.
- The company has a history of promoting primarily from within.
- The company has a strong culture of holding people accountable to plans.

Warning Signs That Borrowing Will Be an Uphill Battle

- CoreCo perceives that NewCo will cannibalize CoreCo revenues.
- CoreCo perceives that NewCo could render a CoreCo competence obsolete.
- CoreCo perceives that NewCo might damage CoreCo assets, such as brands or customer relationships.
- NewCo's losses are rising, even as its leaders are succeeding in growing revenues, and CoreCo managers are questioning the wisdom of allocating capital to a business incurring a loss. Bonuses tied to corporate profits exacerbate the situation.
- Resources are scarce or becoming scarcer as CoreCo goes through a downturn. CoreCo is resistant to allocating capital, manufacturing capacity, employee time, and other resources for NewCo.

- CoreCo managers are unfamiliar with the varying needs of units at different stages in the business life cycle, such as the need to evaluate business performance differently, the need to place more emphasis on flexibility than on efficiency, and the need to hire, promote, and compensate based on unique criteria. In fact, if NewCo managers receive large bonuses when NewCo succeeds, CoreCo may specifically resent the fact that NewCo's success was dependent upon CoreCo resources.

- Establishing trust between CoreCo and NewCo, two very different organizations, is proving difficult.

- CoreCo managers are jealous of NewCo. This is likely if NewCo starts to receive strong public endorsements from analysts, the press, outside consultants, or the CEO. CoreCo managers have worked for years or decades to advance within CoreCo, and now CoreCo may appear inferior to a much younger and sexier division.

- Stereotypes persist about the capabilities of new and old companies. NewCo may assume that big companies cannot be agile or entrepreneurial, and CoreCo may insist that status should be based solely on resources under command. Such attitudes rarely constitute healthy rivalry—and they can easily disrupt cooperation.

- CoreCo is so disciplined about process efficiency that it refuses to alter any processes on NewCo's behalf.

Warning Signs That Learning Will Be an Uphill Battle

- NewCo's leader perceives that NewCo is in a tremendous rush to get to market first—and therefore has little time for planning.
- The company has a tradition of very detailed and exact planning.
- The company has a history of insisting on common planning approaches for every business unit.
- Data on NewCo's performance (other than financials) are difficult to gather or highly ambiguous.
- The nature of NewCo's business is such that it demands major onetime commitments and thus has little opportunity to change direction.
- The company strongly penalizes managers who fail to make their numbers.
- One or more measures of business performance are viewed as important throughout the company. Senior executives judge NewCo by the same measures, even though the measures are probably irrelevant to NewCo.

Originally published in May 2005
Reprint R0505C

Discovery-Driven Planning

RITA GUNTHER MCGRATH AND

IAN C. MACMILLAN

Executive Summary

MANY COMPANIES have used activity-based costing in onetime profitability studies. But when companies integrate ABC into critical management systems and use it to make day-to-day decisions— when they use it as *activity-based management*—it becomes a powerful tool for continuously rethinking and improving a business.

Most managers do not realize that implementing activity-based management is a major organizational-change effort that involves a tremendous amount of work. The biggest obstacle is resistance from employees. The authors focus on two companies—Chrysler Corporation and Safety-Kleen Corporation—whose success in implementing activity-based management can serve as a model for other companies. The benefits they have reaped have been 10 to 20 times their investments in their programs.

Both companies persuaded critical employees, such as plant managers, to give activity-based management a try, then used their success to persuade others. They tackled ongoing business problems to show, rather than tell, employees how activity-based management could expand the business and, as a result, jobs. Both began with one plant, then methodically rolled the system out into the entire organization, involving local managers at each stage. Both invested in educating employees at all levels in the principles and mechanics of activity-based management. And once it had been introduced at a work site, both quickly dumped the old accounting system.

Business lore is full of stories about smart companies that incur huge losses when they enter unknown territory—new alliances, new markets, new products, new technologies. The Walt Disney Company's 1992 foray into Europe with its theme park had accumulated losses of more than $1 billion by 1994. Zapmail, a fax product, cost Federal Express Corporation $600 million before it was dropped. Polaroid lost $200 million when it ventured into instant movies. Why do such efforts often defeat even experienced, smart companies? One obvious answer is that strategic ventures are inherently risky: The probability of failure simply comes with the territory. But many failures could be prevented or their cost contained if senior managers approached innovative ventures with the right planning and control tools.

Discovery-driven planning is a practical tool that acknowledges the difference between planning for a new venture and planning for a more conventional line of business. Conventional planning operates on the premise that managers can extrapolate future results from a well-understood and predictable platform of past experience. One expects predictions to be accurate because they are based on solid knowledge rather than on assumptions. In platform-based planning, a venture's deviations from plan are a bad thing.

The platform-based approach may make sense for ongoing businesses, but it is sheer folly when applied to new ventures. By definition, new ventures call for a company to envision what is unknown, uncertain, and not yet obvious to the competition. The safe, reliable, predictable knowledge of the well-understood business has not yet emerged. Instead, managers must make do with assumptions about the possible futures on which new businesses are based. New ventures are undertaken with a high ratio of assumption to knowledge. With ongoing businesses, one expects the ratio to be the exact opposite. Because assumptions about the unknown generally turn out to be wrong, new ventures inevitably experience deviations—often huge ones—from their original planned targets. Indeed, new ventures frequently require fundamental redirection.

Rather than trying to force startups into the planning methodologies for existing predictable and well-understood businesses, discovery-driven planning acknowledges that at the start of a new venture, little is known and much is assumed. When platform-based planning is used, assumptions underlying a plan are treated as facts—givens to be baked into the plan—rather than as best-guess estimates to be tested and questioned. Companies then forge ahead on the basis of those buried assumptions. In contrast, discovery-driven planning systematically converts assumptions into knowledge as a strategic venture unfolds. When new data are uncovered, they are incorporated into the evolving plan. The real potential of the venture is discovered as it develops—hence the term discovery-driven planning. The approach imposes disciplines different from, but no less precise than, the disciplines used in conventional planning.

Euro Disney and the Platform-Based Approach

Even the best companies can run into serious trouble if they don't recognize the assumptions buried in their plans. The Walt Disney Company, a 49% owner of Euro Disney (now called Disneyland Paris), is known as an astute manager of theme parks. Its success has not been confined to the United States: Tokyo Disneyland has been a financial and public relations success almost from its opening in 1983. Euro Disney is another story, however. By 1993, attendance approached 1 million visitors each month, making the park Europe's most popular paid tourist destination. Then why did it lose so much money?

In planning Euro Disney in 1986, Disney made projections that drew on its experience from its other parks. The company expected half of the revenue to come from admissions, the other half from hotels, food, and merchandise. Although by 1993, Euro Disney had succeeded in reaching its target of 11 million admissions, to do so it had been forced to drop adult ticket prices drastically. The average spending per visit was far below plan and added to the red ink.

The point is not to play Monday-morning quarterback with Disney's experience but to demonstrate an approach that could have revealed flawed assumptions and mitigated the resulting losses. The discipline of systematically identifying key assumptions would have highlighted the business plan's vulnerabilities. Let us look at each source of revenue in turn.

ADMISSIONS PRICE

In Japan and the United States, Disney found its price by raising it over time, letting early visitors go back home and talk up the park to their neighbors. But the planners of Euro Disney assumed that they could hit their target number of visitors even if they started out with an admission price of more than $40 per adult. A major recession in Europe and the determination of the French government to keep the franc strong exacerbated the problem and led to low attendance. Although companies cannot control macroeconomic events, they can highlight and test their pricing assumptions. Euro Disney's prices were very high compared with those of other theme attractions in Europe, such as the aqua palaces, which charged low entry fees and allowed visitors to build their own menus by paying for each attraction individually. By 1993, Euro Disney not only had been forced to make a sharp price reduction to secure its target visitors, it had also lost the benefits of early-stage word of mouth. The talking-up phenomenon is especially important in Europe, as Disney could have gauged from the way word of mouth had benefited Club Med.

HOTEL ACCOMMODATIONS

Based on its experience in other markets, Disney assumed that people would stay an average of four days in the park's five hotels. The average stay in 1993 was only two days. Had the assumption been highlighted, it might have been challenged: Since Euro Disney opened with only 15 rides, compared with 45 at Disney World, people could do them all in a single day.

FOOD

Park visitors in the United States and Japan "graze" all day. At Euro Disney, the buried assumption was that Europeans would do the same. Euro Disney's restaurants, therefore, were designed for all-day streams of grazers. When floods of visitors tried to follow the European custom of dining at noon, Disney was unable to seat them. Angry visitors left the park to eat, and they conveyed their anger to their friends and neighbors back home.

MERCHANDISE

Although Disney did forecast lower sales per visitor in Europe than in the United States and Japan, the company assumed that Europeans would buy a similar mix of cloth goods and print items. Instead, Euro Disney fell short of plan when visitors bought a far smaller proportion of high-margin items such as T-shirts and hats than expected. Disney could have tested the buried assumption before forecasting sales: Disney's retail stores in European cities sell many fewer of the high-margin cloth items and far more of the low-margin print items.

Disney is not alone. Other companies have paid a significant price for pursuing platform-based ventures built on implicit assumptions that turn out to be faulty. Such ventures are usually undertaken without careful up-front identification and validation of those assumptions, which often are unconscious. We have repeatedly observed that the following four planning errors are characteristic of this approach:

Companies don't have hard data but, once a few key decisions are made, proceed as though their assumptions were facts. Euro Disney's implicit assumptions regarding the way visitors would use hotels and restaurants are good examples.

Companies have all the hard data they need to check assumptions but fail to see the implications. After making assumptions based on a subset of the available data, they proceed without ever testing those assumptions. Federal Express based Zapmail on the assumption that there would be a substantial demand for four-hour delivery of documents faxed from FedEx center to FedEx center. What went unchallenged was the implicit assumption that customers would not be able to afford their own fax machines before long. If that assumption had been unearthed, FedEx would have been more likely to take into account the plunging prices and increasing sales of fax machines for the office and, later, for the home.

Companies possess all the data necessary to determine that a real opportunity exists but make implicit and inappropriate assumptions about their ability to implement their plan. Exxon lost $200 million on its office automation business by implicitly assuming that it could build a direct sales and service support capability to compete head-to-head with IBM and Xerox.

Companies start off with the right data, but they implicitly assume a static environment and thus fail to notice until too late that a key variable has changed. Polaroid lost $200 million from Polavision instant movies by assuming that a three minute cassette costing $7 would compete effectively against a half-hour videotape costing $20. Polaroid implicitly assumed that the high cost of equipment for videotaping and playback would remain prohibitive for most consumers. Meanwhile, companies pursuing those technologies steadily drove down costs. (See the exhibit "Some Dangerous Implicit Assumptions.")

Some Dangerous Implicit Assumptions

1. Customers will buy our product because we think it's a good product.
2. Customers will buy our product because it's technically superior.
3. Customers will agree with our perception that the product is "great."
4. Customers run no risk in buying from us instead of continuing to buy from their past suppliers.
5. The product will sell itself.
6. Distributors are desperate to stock and service the product.
7. We can develop the product on time and on budget.
8. We will have no trouble attracting the right staff.
9. Competitors will respond rationally.
10. We can insulate our product from competition.
11. We will be able to hold down prices while gaining share rapidly.
12. The rest of our company will gladly support our strategy and provide help as needed.

Discovery-Driven Planning: An Illustrative Case

Discovery-driven planning offers a systematic way to uncover the dangerous implicit assumptions that would otherwise slip unnoticed and thus unchallenged into the plan. The process imposes a strict discipline that is captured in four related documents: a *reverse income statement,* which models the basic economics of the business; *pro forma operations specs,* which lay out the operations needed to run the business; a *key assumptions checklist,* which is used to ensure that assumptions are checked; and a *milestone planning chart,* which specifies the assumptions to be tested at each project milestone. As the venture unfolds and new data are uncovered, each of the documents is updated.

To demonstrate how this tool works, we will apply it retrospectively to Kao Corporation's highly successful entry into the floppy disk business in 1988. We deliberately draw on no inside information about Kao or its planning process but instead use the kind of limited public knowledge that often is all that any company would have at the start of a new venture.

THE COMPANY

Japan's Kao Corporation was a successful supplier of surfactants to the magnetic-media (floppy disk) industry. In 1981, the company began to study the potential for becoming a player in floppy disks by leveraging the surfactant technology it had developed in its core businesses, soap and cosmetics. Kao's managers realized that they had learned enough process knowledge from their floppy disk customers to supplement their own skills in surface chemistry. They believed they could produce floppy disks at a much lower cost and higher quality than other companies offered at that time. Kao's surfactant competencies were particularly valuable because the quality of the floppy disk's surface is crucial for its reliability. For a company in a mature industry, the opportunity to move current product into a growth industry was highly attractive.

THE MARKET

By the end of 1986, the demand for floppy disks was 500 million in the United States, 100 million in Europe, and 50 million in Japan, with growth estimated at 40% per year, compounded. This meant that by 1993, the global market would be approaching 3 billion disks, of which about a third would be in the original equipment manufacturer (OEM) market, namely such big-volume purchasers of disks as IBM, Apple, and Microsoft, which use disks to distribute their software. OEM industry prices were expected to be about 180 yen per disk by 1993. Quality and reliability have always been important product characteristics for OEMs such as software houses because defective disks have a devastating impact on customers' perceptions of the company's overall quality.

THE REVERSE INCOME STATEMENT

Discovery-driven planning starts with the bottom line. For Kao, back when it began to consider its options, the question was whether the floppy disk venture had the potential to enhance the company's competitive position and financial performance significantly. If not, why should Kao incur the risk and uncertainty of a major strategic venture?

Here, we impose the first discipline, which is to plan
the venture using a reverse income statement, which runs
from the bottom line up. (See the exhibit "First, Start
with a Reverse Income Statement." The four exhibits
referred to in the article are located in the insert "How
Kao Might Have Tackled its New Venture" at the end of
this article) Instead of starting with estimates of revenues
and working down the income statement to derive profits, we start with *required profits.* We then work our way
up the profit and loss to determine how much revenue it
will take to deliver the level of profits we require and how
much cost can be allowed. The underlying philosophy is
to impose revenue and cost disciplines by baking profitability into the plan at the outset: Required profits equal
necessary revenues minus allowable costs.

At Kao in 1988, management might have started with
these figures: net sales, about 500 billion yen; income
before taxes, about 40 billion yen; and return on sales
(ROS), 7.5%. Given such figures, how big must the floppy
disk opportunity be to justify Kao's attention? Every company will set its own hurdles. We believe that a strategic
venture should have the potential to enhance total profits
by at least 10%. Moreover, to compensate for the increased
risk, it should deliver greater profitability than reinvesting
in the existing businesses would. Again, for purposes of
illustration, assume that Kao demands a risk premium
of 33% greater profitability. Since Kao's return on sales
is 7.5%, it will require 10%.

If we use the Kao data, we find that the required profit
for the floppy disk venture would be 4 billion yen (10% × 40
billion). To deliver 4 billion yen in profit with a 10% return
on sales implies a business with 40 billion yen in sales.

Assuming that, despite its superior quality, Kao will
have to price competitively to gain share as a new entrant,

it should set a target price of 160 yen per disk. That translates into unit sales of 250 million disks (40 billion yen in sales divided by 160 yen per disk). By imposing these simple performance measures at the start (1988), we quickly establish both the scale and scope of the venture: Kao would need to capture 25% of the total world OEM market (25% of 1 billion disks) by 1993. Given what is known about the size of the market, Kao clearly must be prepared to compete globally from the outset, making major commitments not only to manufacturing but also to selling.

Continuing up the profit and loss, we next calculate allowable costs: If Kao is to capture 10% margin on a price of 160 yen per disk, the total cost to manufacture, sell, and distribute the disks worldwide cannot exceed 144 yen per disk. The reverse income statement makes clear immediately that the challenge for the floppy disk venture will be to keep a lid on expenses.

THE PRO FORMA OPERATIONS SPECS AND THE ASSUMPTIONS CHECKLIST

The second discipline in the process is to construct pro forma operations specs laying out the activities required to produce, sell, service, and deliver the product or service to the customer. Together, those activities comprise the venture's allowable costs. At first, the operations specs can be modeled on a simple spreadsheet without investing in more than a few telephone calls or on-line searches to get basic data. If an idea holds together, it is possible to identify and test underlying assumptions, constantly fleshing out and correcting the model in light of new information. When a company uses this cumulative approach, major flaws in the business concept soon become obvious, and poor concepts can be abandoned long before significant investments are made.

We believe it is essential to use industry standards for building a realistic picture of what the business has to look like to be competitive. Every industry has its own pressures—which determine normal rates of return in that industry—as well as standard performance measures such as asset-to-sales ratios, industry profit margins, plant utilization, and so on. In a globally competitive environment, no sane manager should expect to escape the competitive discipline that is captured and measured in industry standards. These standards are readily available from investment analysts and business information services. In countries with information sources that are less well developed than those in the United States, key industry parameters are still used by investment bankers and, more specifically, by those commercial bankers who specialize in loans to the particular industry. For those getting into a new industry, the best approach is to adapt standards from similar industries.

Note that we do not begin with an elaborate analysis of product or service attributes or an in-depth market study. That comes later. Initially, we are simply trying to capture the venture's embedded assumptions. The basic discipline is to spell out clearly and realistically where the venture will have to match existing industry standards and in what one or two places managers expect to excel and how they expect to do so.

Kao's managers in 1988 might have considered performance standards for the floppy disk industry. Because there would be no reason to believe that Kao could use standard production equipment any better than established competitors could, it would want to plan to match industry performance on measures relating to equipment use. Kao would ascertain, for example, that the effective production capacity per line was 25 disks per minute in the industry; and the effective life of production equipment was three years. Kao's advantage was in surface chemistry and surface physics, which could improve quality and reduce the cost of materials, thus improving margins. When Kao planned its materials cost, it would want to turn that advantage into a specific challenge for manufacturing: Beat the industry standard for materials cost by 25%. The formal framing of operational challenges is an important step in discovery-driven planning. In our experience, people who are good in design and operations can be galvanized by clearly articulated challenges. That was the case at Canon, for example, when Keizo Yamaji challenged the engineers to develop a personal copier that required minimal service and cost less than $1,000, and the Canon engineers rose to the occasion.

A company can test the initial assumptions against experience with similar situations, the advice of experts in the industry, or published information sources. The point is not to demand the highest degree of accuracy but to build a reasonable model of the economics and logistics of the venture and to assess the order of magnitude of the challenges. Later, the company can analyze where the plan is most sensitive to wrong assumptions and do more formal checks. Consultants to the industry—bankers, suppliers, potential customers, and distributors—often can provide low-cost and surprisingly accurate information.

The company must build a picture of the activities that are needed to carry out the business and the costs. Hence in the pro forma operations specs, we ask how many orders are needed to deliver 250 million units in sales; then how many sales calls it will take to secure those orders; then how many salespeople it will take to make the sales calls, given the fact that they are selling to a global OEM market; then how much it will cost in sales-force compensation. (See the exhibit "Second, Lay Out All the Activities Needed to Run the Venture" located on the sidebar "How Kao Might Have Tackled its New Venture.") Each assumption can be checked, at first somewhat roughly and then with increasing precision. Readers might disagree with our first-cut estimates. That is fine—so might Kao Corporation. Reasonable disagreement triggers discussion and, perhaps, adjustments to the spreadsheet. The evolving document is doing its job if it becomes the catalyst for such discussion.

The third discipline of discovery-driven planning is to compile an assumption checklist to ensure that each assumption is flagged, discussed, and checked as the venture unfolds. (See the exhibit "Third, Track All Assumptions.")

The entire process is looped back into a revised reverse income statement, in which one can see if the entire business proposition hangs together. (See the exhibit "Fourth, Revise the Reverse Income Statement.") If it doesn't, the process must be repeated until the performance requirements and industry standards can be met; otherwise, the venture should be scrapped.

MILESTONE PLANNING

Conventional planning approaches tend to focus managers on meeting plan, usually an impossible goal for a venture rife with assumptions. It is also counterproductive—insistence on meeting plan actually prevents learning. Managers can formally plan to learn by using milestone events to test assumptions.

Milestone planning is by now a familiar technique for monitoring the progress of new ventures. The basic idea, as described by Zenas Block and Ian C. MacMillan in the book *Corporate Venturing* (Harvard Business School Press, 1993), is to postpone major commitments of resources until the evidence from the previous milestone event signals that the risk of taking the next step is justified. What we are proposing here is an expanded use of the tool to support the discipline of transforming assumptions into knowledge.

Going back to what Kao might have been thinking in 1988, recall that the floppy disk venture would require a 40-billion-yen investment in fixed assets alone. Before investing such a large sum, Kao would certainly have wanted to find ways to test the most critical assumptions underlying the three major challenges of the venture:

- capturing 25% global market share with a 20-yen-per-disk discount and superior quality;

- maintaining at least the same asset productivity as the average competitor and producing a floppy disk at 90% of the estimated total costs of existing competitors; and

- using superior raw materials and applied surface technology to produce superior-quality disks for 20 yen per unit instead of the industry standard of 27 yen per unit.

For serious challenges like those, it may be worth spending resources to create specific milestone events to test the assumptions before launching a 40-billion-yen venture. For instance, Kao might subcontract prototype production so that sophisticated OEM customers could conduct technical tests on the proposed disk. If the prototypes survive the tests, then, rather than rest on the assumption that it can capture significant business at the target price, Kao might subcontract production of a large batch of floppy disks for resale to customers. It could thus test the appetite of the OEM market for price discounting from a newcomer.

Similarly, for testing its ability to cope with the second and third challenges once the Kao prototype has been developed, it might be worthwhile to buy out a small existing floppy disk manufacturer and apply the technology in an established plant rather than try to start up a greenfield operation. Once Kao can demonstrate its ability to produce disks at the required quality and cost in the small plant, it can move ahead with its own full-scale plants.

Deliberate assumption-testing milestones are depicted in the exhibit "Finally, Plan to Test Assumptions at Milestones," which also shows some of the other typical milestones that occur in most major ventures. The assumptions that should be tested at each milestone are listed with appropriate numbers from the assumption checklist.

In practice, it is wise to designate a *keeper of the assumptions*—someone whose formal task is to ensure that assumptions are checked and updated as each milestone is reached and that the revised assumptions are incorporated into successive iterations of the four discovery-driven planning documents. Without a specific person dedicated to following up, it is highly unlikely that individuals, up to their armpits in project pressures, will be able to coordinate the updating independently.

Discovery-driven planning is a powerful tool for any significant strategic undertaking that is fraught with uncertainty—new-product or market ventures, technology development, joint ventures, strategic alliances, even major systems redevelopment. Unlike platform-based planning, in which much is known, discovery-driven planning forces managers to articulate what they don't know, and it forces a discipline for learning. As a planning tool, it thus raises the visibility of the make-or-break uncertainties common to new ventures and helps managers address them at the lowest possible cost.

How Kao Might Have Tackled its New Venture: Discovery-Driven Planning in Action

THE GOAL HERE is to determine the value of success quickly. If the venture can't deliver significant returns, it may not be worth the risk.

Keeping a checklist is an important discipline to ensure that each assumption is flagged and tested as a venture unfolds.

Now, with better data, one can see if the entire business proposition hangs together.

First, Start with a Reverse Income Statement

Total Figures
Required profits to add 10% to total profits = 4 billion yen
Necessary revenues to deliver 10% sales margin = 40 billion yen
Allowable costs to deliver 10% sales margin = 36 billion yen

Per Unit Figures
Required unit sales at 160 yen per unit = 250 million units
Necessary percentage of world market share of OEM unit sales = 25%
Allowable costs per unit for 10% sales margin = 144 yen

Second, Lay Out All the Activities Needed to Run the Venture

Pro Forma Operations Specs

1. Sales
Required disk sales = 250 million disks
Average order size (Assumption 8) = 10,000 disks
Orders required (250 million/10,000) = 25,000

Number of calls to make a sale (Assumption 9) = 4
Sales calls required (4 x 25,000) = 100,000 per year

Calls per day per salesperson (Assumption 10) = 2
Annual salesperson days (100,000/2) = 50,000
Sales force for 250 days per year (Assumption 11)
   50,000 salesperson days/250 = 200 people

Salary per salesperson = 10 million yen (Assumption 12)
   Total sales-force salary cost (10 million yen x 200) = 2 billion yen

2. Manufacturing
Quality specification of disk surface: 50% fewer flaws than
   best competitor (Assumption 15)

Annual production capacity per line = 25 per minute x 1440 minutes per day
   x 348 days (Assumption 16) = 12.5 million disks
Production lines needed (250 million disks/12.5 million disks per line) = 20 lines

Production staffing (30 per line [Assumption 17] x 20 lines) = 600 workers
Salary per worker = 5 million yen (Assumption 18)
Total production salaries (600 x 5 million yen) = 3 billion yen

Materials costs per disk = 20 yen (Assumption 19)
Total materials cost (20 x 250 million disks) = 5 billion yen

Packaging per 10 disks = 40 yen (Assumption 20)
Total packaging costs (40 x 25 million packages) = 1 billion yen

3. Shipping
Containers needed per order of 10,000 disks = 1 (Assumption 13)
Shipping cost per container = 100,000 yen (Assumption 14)
Total shipping costs (25,000 orders x 100,000 yen) = 2.5 billion yen

4. Equipment and Depreciation
Fixed asset investment to sales = 1:1 (Assumption 5) = 40 billion yen
Equipment life = 3 years (Assumption 7)
Annual depreciation (40 billion yen/3 years) = 13.3 billion yen

Third, Track All Assumptions

Assumption	Measurement
1. Profit margin	10% of sales
2. Revenues	40 billion yen
3. Unit selling price	160 yen
4. 1993 world OEM market	1 billion disks
5. Fixed asset investment to sales	1:1
6. Effective production capacity per line	25 disks per minute
7. Effective life of equipment	3 years
8. Average OEM order size	10,000 disks
9. Sales calls per OEM order	4 calls per order
10. Sales calls per salesperson per day	2 calls per day
11. Selling days per year	250 days
12. Annual salesperson's salary	10 million yen
13. Containers required per order	1 container
14. Shipping cost per container	100,000 yen
15. Quality level needed to get customers to switch: % fewer flaws per disk than top competitor	50%
16. Production days per year	348 days
17. Workers per production line per day (10 per line for 3 shifts)	30 per line
18. Annual manufacturing worker's salary	5 million yen
19. Materials costs per disk	20 yen
20. Packaging costs per 10 disks	40 yen
21. Allowable administration costs (See revised reverse income statement, below)	9.2 billion yen

Fourth, Revise the Reverse Income Statement

Required margin	10% return on sales
Required profit	4 billion yen
Necessary revenues	40 billion yen
Allowable costs	36 billion yen
Sales-force salaries	2.0 billion yen
Manufacturing salaries	3.0 billion yen
Disk materials	5.0 billion yen
Packaging	1.0 billion yen
Shipping	2.5 billion yen
Depreciation	13.3 billion yen
Allowable administration and overhead costs	9.2 billion yen (Assumption 21)
Per-unit figures	
Selling price	160 yen
Total costs	144 yen
Disk materials costs	20 yen

Finally, Plan to Test Assumptions at Milestones

Milestone event—namely, the completion of:	Assumptions to be tested
1. Initial data search and preliminary feasibility analysis	4: 1993 world OEM market 8: Average OEM order size 9: Sales calls per OEM order 10: Sales calls per salesperson per day 11: Salespeople needed for 250 selling days per year 12: Annual salesperson's salary 13: Containers required per order 14: Shipping cost per container 16: Production days per year 18: Annual manufacturing worker's salary
2. Prototype batches produced	15: Quality to get custmers to switch 19: Materials costs per disk
3. Technical testing by customers	3: Unit selling price 15: Quality to get customers to switch
4. Subcontracted production	19: Materials costs per disk
5. Sales of subcontracted production	1: Profit margin 2: Revenues 3: Unit selling price 8: Average OEM order size 9: Sales calls per saleperson per day 12: Annual sales person's salary 15: Quality to get customers to switch
6. Purchase of an existing plant	5: Fixed assest investment to sales 7: Effective life of equipment
7. Pilot production at purchased plant	6: Effective production capacity per line 16: Production days per year 17: workers per production line per day 18: Annual manufacturing worker's salary 19: Materials cost per disk 20: Packaging cost per 10 disks
8. Competitor reaction	1: Profit margin 2: Revenues 3: Unit selling price
9. Product redesign	19: Materials cost per disk 20: Packaging cost per 10 disks
10. Major repricing analysis	1: Profit margin 2: Revenues 3: Unit selling price 4: 1993 world OEM market
11. Plant redesign	5: Fixed assest investment to sales 6: Effective production capacity per line 3: Materials costs per disk

Note

The authors wish to thank Shiuchi Matsuda of Waseda University's Entrepreneurial Research Unit for providing case material on Kao's floppy disk venture.

Originally published in July 1995
Reprint 95406

Mapping Your Innovation Strategy

SCOTT D. ANTHONY, MATT EYRING,
AND LIB GIBSON

Executive Summary

IN THE COMPLEX SPORT of American football,
teams rely on playbooks as thick as the Manhattan
phone directory. But when it comes to creating
innovative growth businesses—which is at least
as complicated as professional football—most
companies have not developed detailed game
plans. Indeed, many managers have concluded
that a fog enshrouds the world of innovation,
obscuring high-potential opportunities.

The authors believe that companies can penetrate
that fog by developing growth strategies based on
disruptive innovations, as defined by Clayton Christensen. Such innovations conform to a pattern: They
offer an entirely new solution; they perform adequately along traditional dimensions and much

better along other dimensions that matter more to target customers; and they are not initially appealing to powerful incumbents.

Companies can develop customized checklists, or playbooks, by combining this basic pattern with analysis of major innovations in their markets. The key early on is to focus not on detailed financial estimates—which will always guide companies toward the markets most hostile to disruptive innovations—but on how well the innovation fits the pattern of success. It's also crucial to encourage flexibility: Companies must be willing to kill projects that are going nowhere, exempt innovations from standard development processes, and avoid burdening project teams with extra financing, which can keep them heading in the wrong direction.

Companies can create competitive advantage by becoming champions at defining the pattern of successful innovations and executing against it. But as that pattern becomes obvious—and others emerge—building a sustainable advantage on innovation competencies will again prove elusive.

To a casual observer, American football seems pretty simple: You run, you pass, you kick, you pause an inordinate number of times for car commercials. However, any aficionado knows that football is, in reality, dizzyingly complex. A professional team's playbook looks about as thick as the Manhattan phone book. On any given down, the coach selects a formation and a specific play to run from that formation. All the players know their precise assignments for each play and how to adjust them if necessary.

Good coaches know the keys to winning consistently in ever changing circumstances. They need great playbooks that exploit the strengths of their rosters. They need to select plays on the basis of their opponents' strengths and weaknesses and the circumstances of each game. They must be prepared to adjust their game plans midstream. Players need to be flexible, too, ready to change on the fly in reaction to moves by their opponents. Teams that can accomplish these things, week after week of a grueling schedule, emerge as champions.

Most managers would grant that creating innovative growth businesses is at least as complicated as professional football. Yet all too many companies approach innovation without a game plan that positions them for success. Instead, they take the strategies that worked in the past and try to execute them better. Or they fumble in their search for markets that might welcome the technologies incubating in their labs. Ultimately, many companies come to some uneasy realizations: Their old plays are no longer effective. Their unsystematic efforts to create growth lead to random and often disappointing results. After repeated struggles, some managers throw their hands up and declare that bringing predictability to innovation is impossible. Indeed, there is a general sense that a fog enshrouds the world of innovation, obscuring high-potential opportunities and making success a hit-or-miss affair.

It doesn't have to be that way. Over the past five years, we've helped dozens of companies apply Harvard Business School professor Clayton Christensen's insights into disruptive innovation. Our work suggests that a few simple principles can help companies speed through the fuzzy front end of innovation. By creating a playbook for new growth, using it to identify the best opportunities, investing a little to learn a lot, and changing the corporate discourse, companies can develop a process that produces high-quality innovations more quickly and with much less up-front investment.

Pick Your Playing Field

Before deciding *how* to play the innovation game, companies have to decide *where* to play. The good news is that, unlike professional sports teams that go where the schedule makers dictate, companies can choose to play in many different markets. But that is also the bad news. Too much choice can be overwhelming. And the innovation process can slow to a crawl if managers pursue opportunities that don't have a realistic chance of seeing the light of day.

One way to narrow down choices is to clarify what the company *won't* do. For example, a newspaper company that was looking into the wireless market set strict boundaries: no gaming, no gambling, and no personal ads. The company knew those boundaries left promising growth opportunities on the table, but they also kept middle managers from wasting time on ideas that senior managers would ultimately kill.

Paradoxically, these kinds of constraints can be liberating, helping to focus managers' creative energy. The search for new growth, however, can still be daunting. Most companies intuitively sense that the best place to look for growth is outside of—but not too far from—their core business. But where? We believe that strategies based on disruptive innovations have the highest chances of creating growth. Generally speaking, these innovations offer lower performance along dimensions that incumbent firms consider critical. In exchange, they introduce benefits such as simplicity, convenience, ease of use, and low prices. To spot markets that have a high potential for a disruptive approach, we ask three basic questions. (For a closer look at the three questions, see the insert "The Disruptive Playbook" at the end of this article.)

WHAT JOBS CAN'T OUR EXISTING CUSTOMERS GET DONE?

As Christensen has pointed out, when customers buy products, they are in essence hiring them to get important jobs done. Companies can start the search for growth opportunities by examining why customers hire their current products. That understanding can point to related jobs that customers can't get done.

Consider how software provider Intuit developed the insight that led to its massively successful QuickBooks package. In the early 1990s, Intuit observed that many people who used Quicken, the company's personal financial software, were small-business owners. That was curious because Intuit hadn't designed the software to manage a business. The company realized that the job these customers had to get done was a simple one: Make sure I don't run out of cash. Software programs such as Peachtree that were designed for the small-business market were generally packed with complicated functions like depreciation schedules, which small-business owners found unnecessary and intimidating. Intuit realized that users enjoyed Quicken's simplicity and easy-to-navigate user interface. Intuit adapted that program for small-business owners, branded it under the QuickBooks name, and quickly became the dominant player in the category. "We uncovered a giant opportunity," Intuit cofounder Scott Cook said. "The majority of small-business people do not have the skill to utilize debit- and credit-based software, but they have to keep books."

As the Intuit example shows, it's important to notice if your customers are using existing products in unusual ways, stretching them to do something they were not designed for, or "kludging" several together for a suboptimal solution. Those compensating behaviors signal that customers do not have access to the ideal product. None of the solutions small-business owners hired for the "don't run out of cash" job—pen and paper, Quicken, Excel spreadsheets—were a perfect fit, which spelled opportunity for innovation.

WHO ARE THE INDUSTRY'S WORST CUSTOMERS?

An industry's worst customers might sound like the last place to look for new growth. But thinking about ways to serve seemingly undesirable customers can point to novel strategies. Global silicone leader Dow Corning, for example, found a successful growth strategy by focusing on the low end of its customer base. The company produces the world's highest-quality silicones, used in applications ranging from shampoos to space shuttles. Dow Corning's scientists provide high value-added services to its customers. Yet the company found that its traditional business model actually overshot the needs of customers looking for basic silicones at reasonable prices. Those seemingly unattractive customers were turning to low-cost competitors that provided less-advanced products and no-frills service.

As the industry's largest player, Dow Corning would be able to take advantage of scale economics to play in this tier of the market—if it could reconstitute its business model. In 2002, it launched a distribution channel called Xiameter, designed to compete at the commodity end of the silicone business. By embracing a business model that differs sharply from its core model, Dow Corning is prospering in a very challenging market space.

WHERE ARE THERE BARRIERS THAT CONSTRAIN CONSUMPTION?

Throughout history, some of the most powerful growth strategies have democratized markets, blowing open select groups of the few, the trained, and the wealthy and thereby dramatically expanding consumption. Companies should scan for markets limited in various ways. Sometimes markets are constrained because products are too expensive for mass consumption. Sometimes the need for expertise limits a market to those with special training. Sometimes the need to go to a centralized setting, such as having to go to a doctor's office for a diagnosis, makes it difficult for individuals who prefer to "do it themselves."

Looking for such pools of bottled-up consumption led Turner Broadcasting System, a multibillion-dollar subsidiary of Time Warner, to a counterintuitive growth strategy. All of Turner's successes had been cable channels, like Cable News Network (CNN), Turner Classic Movies (TCM), and the Cartoon Network. In each case, the company had succeeded by obtaining basic content at a reasonable price and then shaping and molding it into a differentiated offering.

To find new growth, Turner looked for non-television markets that might have desirable content consumers couldn't easily access. The search led to gaming. Gaming companies had vast stores of content they pulled off the shelves years ago, just like the old movies that air on TCM. A consumer looking for one of those games had to put up with inferior online replications or try to find the original game on eBay—and that option would work only if the consumer owned the console on which the game operated.

Turner's strategy attempted to expand consumption of out-of-circulation games. The company licensed thousands of games—from timeless classics like Pong and Asteroids to more recent hits like Tomb Raider and Splinter Cell—and in 2005 launched a Web-based subscription service called GameTap. Although it is too early to measure results, the company's approach is consistent with other democratizing innovations that have created substantial growth businesses.

Build Your Growth Playbook

Once a company has identified the market space it wishes to target, it's time to look more specifically at how to serve that market. As an example, consider MinuteClinic, an emerging provider of health care diagnostic services. Its kiosks, located in stores such as Target and CVS, offer a menu of services for diagnosing about 25 straightforward ailments, including strep throat and pinkeye. The nurse practitioner who staffs the kiosk can reliably diagnose the conditions in less than 15 minutes and write a prescription that the customer can fill in the in-store pharmacy.

MinuteClinic shares the following characteristics with other disruptive innovations:

- *The target customer is looking for something different because existing solutions are too expensive, too*

complicated, or don't quite get the job done. Minute-Clinic's customers aren't looking for better-trained doctors; they are looking for speed and convenience.

- *The solution is good enough along traditional performance dimensions and superior along other dimensions that matter more to target customers.* MinuteClinic can't treat everything. If a customer comes in and says, "I feel dizzy" or "Something is wrong with me, but I don't know what," MinuteClinic refers the patient to a physician in a traditional setting. But MinuteClinic has better performance along dimensions its customers care about—speed and convenience.

- *The business model has low overhead and high asset utilization, allowing companies to offer low prices or serve small markets.* MinuteClinic, with its lean overhead and effective software systems, can provide a lower-cost solution that is extremely appealing to insurers and corporate sponsors.

- *The strategy is not one that powerful incumbents initially want to pursue themselves.* Many primary care physicians welcome MinuteClinic's solution because it frees them to work on the more complicated problems that are a better fit with their training.

While this basic disruptive pattern holds true across industries, companies need to customize an approach that reflects the idiosyncrasies of their particular markets. Thus they need to develop checklists that spell out the market circumstances where the approach has the best chance of succeeding and identify criteria to which successful strategies should conform.

One way to develop such a checklist is to analyze ten to 15 major innovations in the market segment's history.

Look at both successes and failures, particularly the "sure-fire" strategies that flopped and the "unpromising" ones that were runaway successes. Figure out the elements shared by the truly successful strategies. Combine the results of this historical analysis with the basic disruptive principles, and you have your customized checklist, or playbook. For example, a consumer health care company identified at-home diagnostics as a key growth area. It was interested in understanding why some consumer-based diagnostics, such as pregnancy kits and blood glucose monitors, took off while others, like home drug tests, floundered. By analyzing the history of home diagnostics from a disruptive perspective, the company identified the characteristics shared by successful innovations. It then created a 20-point checklist to assess new products that included elements such as the following:

- Is the diagnostic job important to the consumer?

- Is diagnosing currently very difficult, inconvenient, or expensive?

- Are results conclusive without further testing or triaging of symptoms?

- Is the diagnostic linked to treatment or follow-up action?

- Are we capable of developing the necessary technology?

- Can we communicate effectively to the target consumer?

- Will influencers (such as professional caregivers and insurers) actively support the diagnostic?

- Will our competitors have difficulty duplicating this product?

The checklist allowed the company to look at any opportunity from multiple perspectives, including those of consumers, competitors, the channel, and regulators. The diversity of perspectives allowed the company to avoid a classic trap: a myopic focus on innovation within a company's comfort zone. For example, a firm with a strong engineering culture might focus primarily on whether it can solve a tough technological problem. This kind of focused question is important, but companies that don't also develop a holistic sense of an opportunity run the risk of missing important elements that can come back to bite them.

With these guidelines in hand, companies can then begin to move from generic plays to specific opportunities for innovation.

Build Your Innovation Game Plan

Now it's time to create a short list of innovation ideas for your target market and to assess whether those ideas adhere to the general pattern of success you've uncovered and to your specific checklist.

The discipline of checking seemingly high-potential ideas against a rigorous list of questions should keep you from moving forward with a plan that's similar to something that worked in the past but different in some crucial way. For example, Procter & Gamble has time and again leveraged its massive distribution power to muscle itself into a product category. To take just one example, in 1999 the consumer products giant purchased Iams, a niche pet food provider, for $2.3 billion. By improving an already good product and bringing it to tens of thousands of grocery stores, where it competed against fragmented providers, P&G created a blockbuster brand.

However, when P&G tried to enter the prepackaged cookie market with its Duncan Hines soft-baked cookies in the 1980s, it was a different story. The market was not fragmented, and strong competitors Keebler and Nabisco reacted ferociously to P&G's entry. Although P&G claimed the rivals had infringed its patents (and ultimately won a lawsuit), it had to exit the market. P&G's classic consolidation-and-distribution play worked when competitors were fragmented but failed when two powerful incumbents were among them. A checklist that included questions about the clout of potential competitors might have alerted managers to the problem.

CREATING SPECIFIC OPPORTUNITIES

Let's look in detail at how one company identified, then assessed, a potential innovation. Ethicon Endo-Surgery, a multibillion-dollar company, sells equipment for minimally invasive surgeries. In analyzing the industry's pattern of success, EES managers realized that the most successful new medical devices typically enabled less highly trained (and less costly) practitioners to treat patients themselves instead of referring them to specialists.

EES managers then looked methodically for an existing surgical procedure characterized by a lot of seemingly avoidable high costs. They learned that more than a quarter of colon resections—painful, invasive, high-cost procedures—remove a benign growth. That figure seemed high, so EES managers started talking to leading gastroenterologists, many of whom had a rule of thumb: Any growth of more than two centimeters gets referred to a surgeon because the gastroenterologist can't efficiently remove such polyps, which are often cancerous. Once EES identified this circumstance, which had high potential for a novel approach, it started looking for a specific technology to bring to the market. Some internal brainstorming, followed by an intensive survey of external technologies and development work, led to a project to develop a device that would enable gastroenterologists or clinicians to remove large polyps noninvasively, during a colonoscopy. Clinicians who have used the device say that it has the potential to become the new standard of care, allowing more practitioners to treat patients less invasively and in less centralized settings.

The process of assessing an opportunity against a checklist often leads a company to go ahead with the project—but adjust it in some crucial way to fit the pattern of successful innovations. For example, a team at P&G was evaluating a strategy to bring one of its leading brands to China. The team knew its solution had to be very low cost and still perform adequately along dimensions that consumers cared about. But to get the product to a low enough price point, P&G would need to strip out functionality that demanding consumers in the country's largest cities considered critical. This assessment led P&G to start in smaller Chinese cities, where consumers for whom existing alternatives were too expensive would embrace P&G's limited first-generation product. As P&G works out the inevitable kinks in manufacturing such a low-cost product and improves its functionality, it plans to introduce the product in larger cities.

FOCUSING ON PATTERNS INSTEAD OF NUMBERS

Many seasoned innovators might be asking themselves, "But what about the numbers?" Obviously, when you're planning to launch product or service, you can't ignore

financial data. However, our experience suggests that
most companies force teams to develop detailed financial estimates way too early, when their accuracy will
necessarily be low. Using metrics such as net present
value (NPV) or return on investment (ROI) as rough
guidelines is fine. Using them as rank-ordering tools to
make decisions is counterproductive.

Here's why: Companies that rank projects using
detailed financial metrics won't end up selecting ones
aimed at the seemingly small, difficult-to-measure markets that are so often the footholds for powerful growth
strategies. Instead, they'll likely move forward with
projects in large, measurable markets—the ones that are
usually hostile to disruptive innovations. As a result, new
products often fail to deliver significant, differentiated
new benefits, or the company suffers a devastating
response from incumbents.

Instead of fretting over precise figures, play the "number
of zeros" game. Determine whether the revenue created by
an opportunity will have eight zeros on the end ($100 mil-
lion) or five ($100,000). Focusing on the assumptions
behind those estimates—what must be true for those
estimates to be plausible—is meaningful. Arguing about
whether an opportunity will produce revenues of $23
million or $28 million is pointless at this early stage.

Detailed metrics make sense for product extensions
in known markets. Innovation strategies that are markedly
different need an appropriately different evaluation process. A company's early focus has to be on how well the
innovation fits with the pattern of success. Had the P&G
team mentioned earlier focused on detailed metrics too
soon, it probably would have decided to start in China's
largest cities. After all, that approach would appear to
yield the highest first-year sales and NPV figures. By

paying attention to its playbook, however, the team saw that starting in the big cities would actually lead to failure.

Execute and Adapt

If everything went exactly as coaches diagrammed, football would be a pretty boring game (rugby fans might argue that it already is pretty boring). The result of any play would be perfectly predictable. In reality, however, plays often unfold in completely unanticipated ways. Companies need to make sure that as they begin to execute their new-growth game plans, they, too, encourage adaptation and flexibility. They can do this by following a simple mantra: Invest a little, learn a lot.

Big companies often think their deeper pockets give them an advantage over start-ups. But sometimes extra financing is a curse. Project teams with too much money may keep going in the wrong direction for too long. Those with scarce resources, however, must scramble to find novel approaches that they might not otherwise discover.

One powerful example of this principle is Teradyne's efforts in the late 1990s to create a disruptive product in semiconductor test equipment. Teradyne's CEO at the time, Alex d'Arbeloff, recognized that emerging technologies would allow the company to create machines that were dramatically smaller, cheaper, and simpler to use than the products it currently sold to market leaders like Intel. The new machines wouldn't be as functional, but they might be good enough for some market segments. It felt like a classic case of disruptive innovation.

D'Arbeloff gave the team, code-named Aurora, modest revenue expectations—$1 million in year one and $11 million in year two—but demanded that it achieve profitability before he invested significant sums of money. By constraining the team's financial (and therefore engineering) resources, he forced it to find a foothold market it could attack quickly. The team just didn't have the luxury of spending years in development to make the product good enough for Teradyne's core customers. Although team members occasionally muttered not-so-nice things under their breath about d'Arbeloff, scarcity compelled them to experiment with novel approaches. Ultimately, the team found a surprising way into the market by targeting manufacturers who produced inexpensive commodity semiconductors that perform basic computations in household appliances such as toasters. Historically, these customers couldn't afford Teradyne's expensive, complicated test equipment, but they loved the simpler, cheaper Aurora product. The product took off and created a substantial growth business for Teradyne.

Some managers might be nodding their heads at this point, thinking, "We get this. We have brought the venture capital approach into our organization." Our experience suggests that many companies that think they are following an "invest a little, learn a lot" approach are actually falling into one of three classic traps: They are unwilling to kill projects that have fatal flaws; they commit too much capital too soon, allowing a project team to follow the wrong approach for too long; or they fail to adapt their strategies even in the face of information that suggests their current approach is wrong.

To avoid these mistakes, companies should be rigorous about staging their investments. Early investments should focus on resolving critical unknowns. Identifying where the team should focus is straightforward. Just ask the following questions: What is the consequence of being wrong about an assumption? Is it catastrophic or potentially harmless? How much certainty do I have that

I am right? Enough to bet my job on it? How long would it take and how much would it cost to become more knowledgeable?

By answering these questions and identifying critical assumptions, teams can direct their investments to the appropriate experiments. After running the experiments, companies then have one of four options:

- *Double down:* Information clearly points to a winning strategy with no obvious deal-killing uncertainties, so move forward rapidly.

- *Continue exploring:* All signs look positive, but there are still untested assumptions, so keep experimenting.

- *Adjust the game plan:* Investigation suggests that the current strategy is not viable, but another approach might be, so change the approach and begin experimenting again.

- *Shelve:* There is no clear path forward, so move on to other projects until something else changes.

The key is to make decisions rapidly. We have seen companies seeking to build their innovation capabilities try to move dozens of ideas forward simultaneously. Starting with a lot of ideas is important, but success requires the fortitude to shut down the unpromising ones and redirect those that are heading in the wrong direction. If companies wait too long to make these decisions, they end up diverting resources toward fruitless efforts or continuing to execute a fatally flawed strategy. Consider the words of a newspaper editor who faced this difficulty as his company attempted to innovate on the Internet: "Given the pace of our expansion, I don't think we made mistakes fast enough, and we didn't learn from them often enough. The problem wasn't just turning [the experiments] on, sometimes it was turning them off."

Change Your Role

It will come as no surprise that senior management has an important role to play in building a strong capability around growth and innovation. Creating a separate pool of resources for growth initiatives and fiercely protecting that pool is one obvious step. But senior managers need to do more than provide resources. They need to shield innovation projects as if they were viruses threatened by corporate antibodies. And they need to work with innovators to solve vexing strategic issues.

BLOCKING THE ANTIBODIES

Consider a chemical company that was working with a wide array of suppliers to quickly bring customized products to the marketplace. The strategy was very different from the one the company used in its core business, where it worked with just a few suppliers and followed a very rigorous and lengthy process to ensure that suppliers met high quality standards. That process worked extremely well when the company was adding another core supplier. However, it crippled the new approach, which focused on mix-and-match, fast customization. By the time a supplier received clearance, a window of opportunity had slammed shut.

With this realization, senior management gave the team "process FastPass" cards modeled on Disney's program that allows people to cut to the front of lines on popular rides. As long as the team had convincing evidence that using a supplier would not get the company in trouble, it could bypass the standard approval process. Fortunately, most of the suppliers in question worked with other industry players and so easily passed that litmus test.

Mobile phone giant Motorola applied a similar principle while developing its ultra-thin Razr phone. Usually, when Motorola planned to develop a new phone, representatives from each of the company's major geographic regions (Europe, Asia, and so on) weighed in on the concept. The regions would request the sorts of features and functions they wanted in the design. Each region would then forecast how many units of the model it thought would sell. The aggregated regional plans would help Motorola decide whether to invest in the phone.

It was always a complicated dance. If a development team ignored features that a specific region deemed critical, that region would project low sales, which would make it tougher for the development team to get approval for the project. Teams knew, then, that they had to appease each of the regions. Although this system ensured that products reflected some critical feedback from the regions, it could force designers to develop compromise products that were acceptable to everyone yet delightful to no one.

With the Razr, Motorola's management sensed an opportunity to buck industry trends. Whereas competitors were racing to cram more features and functionality onto handsets, Motorola decided to limit features and focus on form, creating the smallest, thinnest phone on the market. Luckily, management recognized that it had to buffer the Razr team if it wanted to introduce this blockbuster innovation. Senior management exempted the Razr from the company's standard development process, giving the team freedom to create a novel product that delighted customers and caught competitors off guard. The Razr exceeded the company's total lifetime projections for the product in its first three months, turning into a massive success story for Motorola.

CHANGING THE CONVERSATION

In addition to shielding project teams, senior managers must also change the discourse with them. As more and more companies have adopted stage-gate processes to manage innovation, an us-against-them mentality has emerged. Teams present to senior managers, who then act as gatekeepers, either opening the gate to let projects through or locking it until the team comes back with better numbers or more proof. When the right strategy is unknown and unknowable—as it so often is with novel growth initiatives—senior managers need to be problem solvers, not dictators.

Karl Ronn from P&G embodies this notion. Ronn, the vice president for research and development for the company's home care division, oversees such brands as Mr. Clean, Dawn, Swiffer, and Febreze. When a team is working on an incremental line extension, Ronn receives results at predetermined milestones. But when P&G is developing extremely novel products, such as the Mr. Clean Magic Eraser or Flick (a version of Swiffer that cleans carpets), Ronn acts differently. Instead of reviewing results of agreed-upon decisions, he and the business unit president go into the labs to review early prototypes and participate in daylong brainstorming sessions. Such deeper engagement allows senior managers to get a better feel for the new products and share their collective wisdom with the team. "This is not like a Skunk Works where we cut out the middle managers," Ronn said. "Rather, we are there with them to help and also to learn about the business before we have to invest in it."

Generally, senior managers overseeing novel growth strategies need to engage frequently with the managers developing and implementing them. Quarterly meetings either slow progress or lead teams to make critical decisions without senior management's guidance.

Now, of course senior management can't be deeply engaged in every project. If a project is in a well-known market, it's appropriate for senior management to act as a traditional gatekeeper. Nor should senior managers abdicate their role as decision makers who determine when a team has learned enough to continue moving forward. But if neither management nor the team knows the answer, senior managers ought to break out of the us-versus-them mind-set and use their strategic thinking skills to help the team solve problems. (See the insert "Changing the Innovation Mind-Set" for other important changes.)

Companies can pierce the fog of innovation. An unpredictable innovation process teeming with trade-offs between speed, quality, and investment can become better, faster, and cheaper. By allocating resources more efficiently and accelerating the highest-potential innovations, companies can enjoy a winning streak of innovation successes that will throw competitors off balance.

But the opportunity that now exists to build a competitive advantage through innovation won't last forever. That's because problem-solving approaches evolve in a predictable way. When people first encounter a new type of challenge, they must solve it using an unstructured, trial-and-error approach. Over time, as they learn more about that particular challenge, clear rules emerge to guide problem-solving efforts. We believe that innovation is now somewhere between random trial-and-error and perfectly predictable, paint-by-number rules. We think of this transitional period as the era of pattern recognition, during which companies can create competitive advantage by becoming world-class at defining and executing against patterns. As the patterns we've identified become more obvious—and as others emerge—it will once again become difficult to base a sustainable competitive advantage on innovation competencies. But for the moment, forward-thinking companies can head out in new directions by learning how to see patterns where others see chaos.

The Disruptive Playbook

AT THE CORE of the disruptive innovation theory developed by Harvard Business School professor Clayton Christensen is a simple principle: Companies innovate faster than people's lives change. Most organizations make products that are too good, too expensive, and too inconvenient for many customers. This happens for a good reason. After all, managers are trained to seek higher profits by bringing better products to the most demanding customers. But in the pursuit of profits, companies overshoot less-demanding customers who are perfectly willing to take the basics at reasonable prices. And they ignore nonconsumers who may need to get a job done but lack the skills, wealth, or ability to adopt existing solutions.

Companies seeking to create growth through disruption can run three basic plays, each of which is suited to certain circumstances.

The Back-Scratcher: Scratch an Unscratched Itch

What it is: Make it easier and simpler for people to get an important job done.

When it works best: When customers are frustrated by their inability to get a job done and competitors are either fragmented or have a disability that prevents them from responding.

Historical examples: Federal Express, Intuit's Quick-Books.

Current examples: Procter & Gamble's Swiffer products, instant messaging technology.

The Extreme Makeover: Make an Ugly Business Attractive

What it is: Find a way to prosper at the low end of established markets by giving people good enough solutions at low prices.

When it works best: When target customers don't need and don't value all the performance that can be packed into products and when existing competitors don't focus on low-end customers.

Historical examples: Nucor's steel mini-mill, Toyota Corona.

Current examples: India-based Tata's sub-$3,000 automobile, exchange-traded mutual funds.

The Bottleneck Buster: Democratize a Limited Market

What it is: Expand a market by removing a barrier to consumption.

When it works best: When some customers are locked out of a market because they lack skills, access, or wealth. Competitors ignore initial developments because they take place in seemingly unpromising markets.

Historical examples: Personal computers, balloon angioplasty, Sony Walkman, eBay.

Current examples: Blogs, home diagnostics.

Changing the Innovation Mind-Set

IMPLEMENTING the principles we discuss can allow companies to embrace new innovation mind-sets:

- **Good enough can be great.** Many companies unintentionally slow the innovation process by pushing for perfection. eBay CEO Meg Whitman, quoted in a March 2005 issue of *USA Today,* put in nicely: "It's better to put something out there and see the reaction and fix it on the fly . . . It's another way of saying 'perfect' is the enemy of 'good enough.'"

- **Step, don't leap.** Great leaps forward, when companies spend many years and millions of dollars seeking to jump over existing companies, almost never work. Companies have a much greater chance of success if they start with a simple springboard. Think about the journey of P&G's Febreze brand. P&G initially positioned Febreze as a "removing odor" brand by packaging it to look like other household cleaners and placing it in the laundry aisle next to such powerhouse brands as Tide and Downy. The company then introduced Air Effects, thus moving Febreze toward a "clean the air" brand. In early 2006 P&G introduced Febreze Noticeables, a plug-in air freshener that alternates between two scents. P&G has obviously moved squarely into the air freshening market, but it has done so in a thoughtful, staged way.

- **The right kind of failure is success.** Most well-run companies naturally consider failure to be highly undesirable. But remember, most of the time the initial strategy for a growth business is going to be wrong. Managers need to recognize that learning what's wrong with an approach and adapting appropriately is a good thing, not a failure. The Mayo Clinic gives a "queasy eagle" award to individuals who fail for the right reason. Managers must balance the confidence to start going in an uncertain direction, the humility to recognize that the direction is wrong, and the fortitude to listen, learn, and adapt.

Originally published in May 2006
Reprint R0605F

Finding Your Next Core Business

CHRIS ZOOK

Executive Summary

HOW DO YOU KNOW when your core needs to change? And how do you determine what should replace it? From an in-depth study of 25 companies, the author, a strategy consultant, has discovered that it's possible to measure the vitality of a business's core. If it needs reinvention, he says, the best course is to mine hidden assets.

Some of the 25 companies were in deep crisis when they began the process of redefining themselves. But, says Zook, management teams can learn to recognize early signs of erosion. He offers five diagnostic questions with which to evaluate the customers, key sources of differentiation, profit pools, capabilities, and organizational culture of your core business.

The next step is strategic regeneration. In four-fifths of the companies Zook examined, a hidden asset was the centerpiece of the new strategy. He provides a map for identifying the hidden assets in your midst, which tend to fall into three categories: undervalued business platforms, untapped insights into customers, and underexploited capabilities. The Swedish company Dometic, for example, was manufacturing small absorption refrigerators for boats and RVs when it discovered a hidden asset: its understanding of, and access to, customers in the RV market. The company took advantage of a boom in that market to refocus on complete systems for live-in vehicles. The Danish company Novozymes, which produced relatively low-tech commodity enzymes such as those used in detergents, realized that its underutilized biochemical capability in genetic and protein engineering was a hidden asset and successfully refocused on creating bioengineered specialty enzymes.

Your next core business is not likely to announce itself with fanfare. Use the author's tools to conduct an internal audit of possibilities and pinpoint your new focus.

IT IS A WONDER how many management teams fail to exploit, or even perceive, the full potential of the basic businesses they are in. Company after company prematurely abandons its core in the pursuit of some hot market or sexy new idea, only to see the error of its ways—often when it's too late to reverse course. Bausch &

Lomb is a classic example. Its eagerness to move beyond contact lenses took it into dental products, skin care, and even hearing aids in the 1990s. Today B&L has divested itself of all those businesses at a loss, and is scrambling in the category it once dominated (where Johnson & Johnson now leads). And yet it's also true that no core endures forever. Sticking with an eroding core for too long, as Polaroid did, can be just as devastating. Both these companies were once darlings of Wall Street, each with an intelligent management team and a formerly dominant core. And in a sense, they made the same mistake: They misjudged the point their core business had reached in its life cycle and whether it was time to stay focused, expand, or move on.

How do you know when your core needs to change in some fundamental way? And how do you determine what the new core should be? These are the questions that have driven my conversations with senior managers and the efforts of my research team over the past three years. What we've discovered is that it is possible to measure the vitality remaining in a business's core—to see whether that core is truly exhausted or still has legs. We've also concluded from an in-depth study of companies that have redefined their cores (including Apple, IBM, De Beers, PerkinElmer, and 21 others) that there is a right way to go about reinvention. The surest route is not to venture far afield but to mine new value close to home; assets already in hand but peripheral to the core offer up the richest new cores.

This article discusses both these findings. It identifies the warning signs that a business is losing its potency and offers a way to diagnose the strength remaining in its core. It recounts the efforts of managers in a variety of settings who saw the writing on the wall and succeeded in transforming their companies. And, based on these and other cases, it maps the likely spots in a business where the makings of a new core might be found.

When It's Time for Deep Strategic Change

Not every company that falls on hard times needs to rethink its core strategy. On the contrary, declining performance in what was a thriving business can usually be chalked up to an execution shortfall. But when a strategy does turn out to be exhausted, it's generally for one of three reasons.

The first has to do with *profit pools*—the places along the total value chain of an industry where attractive profits are earned. If your company is targeting a shrinking or shifting profit pool, improving your ability to execute can accomplish only so much. Consider the position of Apple, whose share of the market for personal computers plummeted from 9% in 1995 to less than 3% in 2005. But more to the point, the entire profit pool in PCs steadily contracted during those years. If Apple had not moved its business toward digital music, its prospects might not look very bright. General Dynamics was in a similar situation in the 1990s, when defense spending declined sharply. To avoid being stranded by the receding profit pool, it sold off many of its units and redefined the company around just three core businesses where it held substantial advantages: submarines, electronics, and information systems.

The second reason is *inherently inferior economics*. These often come to light when a new competitor enters the field unburdened by structures and costs that an older company cannot readily shake off. General Motors saw this in competition with Toyota, just as Compaq did with Dell. Other well-known examples include Kmart (vis-à-vis Wal-Mart) and Xerox (vis-à-vis Canon). Occasionally a company sees the clouds gathering and is able to respond effectively. The Port of Singapore Authority (now PSA International), for example, fought off threats from Malaysia and other upstart competitors by slashing costs and identifying new ways to add value for customers. But sometimes the economics are driven by laws or entrenched arrangements that a company cannot change.

The third reason to rethink a core strategy is *a growth formula that cannot be sustained.* A manufacturer of a specialized consumer product—cell phones, say—might find its growth stalling as the market reaches saturation or competitors replicate its once unique source of differentiation. Or a retailer like Home Depot might see its growth slow as competitors like Lowe's catch up. A company that has prospered by simply reproducing its business model may run out of new territory to conquer: Think of the difficulties Wal-Mart has encountered as the cost-benefit ratio of further expansion shifts unfavorably. The core business of a mining company might expire as its mines become depleted. In all such circumstances, finding a new formula for growth depends on finding a new core.

For most of the companies my team and I studied, recognition that the core business had faltered came very late. The optical instruments maker PerkinElmer, the diamond merchant De Beers, the audio equipment manufacturer Harman International—these were all companies in deep crisis when they began their redefinition. Is it inevitable that companies will be blindsided in this way? Or can a management team learn to see early signs that its core strategy is losing relevance?

With that possibility in mind, it would seem reasonable to periodically assess the fundamental vitality of your business. The exhibit "Evaluate Your Core Business" offers a tool for doing so. Its first question looks at the core in terms of the customers it serves. How profitable are they—and how loyal? Arriving at the answers can be difficult, but no undertaking is more worthwhile; strategy goes nowhere unless it begins with the customer. The second question probes your company's key sources of differentiation and asks whether they are strengthening or eroding. The third focuses on your industry's profit pools, a perspective that is often neglected in the quest for revenue and market share growth. Where are the best profits to be found? Who earns them now? How might that change? The fourth examines your company's capabilities—a topic we shall soon turn to— and the fifth assesses your organization's culture and readiness to change.

At the least, managers who go through this exercise tend to spot areas of weakness to be shored up. More dramatically, they may save a business from going under. Note, however, that no scoring system is attached to this diagnostic tool—there is no clearly defined point at which a prescription for strategic redefinition is issued. That would lend false precision to what must be a judgment call by a seasoned management team. The value of the exercise is to ensure that the right questions are taken into account and, by being asked consistently over time, highlight changes that may constitute growing threats to a company's core.

Recognizing the Makings of a New Core

Management teams react in different ways when they reach the conclusion that a core business is under severe

Evaluate Your Core Business

Five broad questions can help you determine when it is time to redefine your company's core business. For most companies, the answers to these questions can be found by examining the categories listed next to each one.

If the answers reveal that large shifts are about to take place in two or more of these five areas, your company is heading into turbulence; you need to reexamine the fundamentals of your core strategy and even the core itself.

Question	Take a close look at
1. What is the state of our core customers?	> profitability > market share > retention rate > measures of customer loyalty and advocacy > share of wallet
2. What is the state of our core differentiation?	> definition and metrics of differentiation > relative cost position > business models of emerging competitors > increasing or decreasing differentiation
3. What is the state of our industry's profit pools?	> size, growth, and stability > share of profit pools captured > boundaries > shifts and projections > high costs and prices
4. What is the state of our core capabilities?	> inventory of key capabilities > relative importance > gaps vis-à-vis competitors and vis-à-vis future core needs
5. What is the state of our culture and organization?	> loyalty and undesired attrition > capacity and stress points > alignment and agreement with objectives > energy and motivation > bottlenecks to growth

threat. Some decide to defend the status quo. Others want to transform their companies all at once through a big merger. Some leap into a hot new market. Such strategies are inordinately risky. (Our analysis suggests that the odds of success are less than one in ten for the first two strategies, and only about one in seven for the third.) The companies we found to be most successful in remaking themselves proceeded in a way that left less to chance. Consider, for example, the transformation of the Swedish company Dometic.

Dometic's roots go back to 1922, when two engineering students named Carl Munters and Baltzar von Platen applied what was known as absorption technology to refrigeration. Whereas most household refrigerators use compressors driven by electric motors to generate cold, their refrigerator had no moving parts and no need for electricity; only a source of heat, as simple as a propane tank, was required. So the absorption refrigerator is particularly useful in places like boats and recreational vehicles, where electric current is hard to come by. In 1925 AB Electrolux acquired the patent rights. The division responsible for absorption refrigerators later became the independent Dometic Group.

By 1973 Dometic was still a small company, with revenues of just 80 million kronor (about U.S. $16.9 million). Worse, it was losing money. Then Sven Stork, an executive charged with fixing the ailing Electrolux product line, began to breathe new life into the business. Stork, who went on to become president and CEO of the company, moved aggressively into the hotel minibar market, where the absorption refrigerator's silent operation had a real advantage over conventional technology. Fueled by those sales, Dometic grew and was able to acquire some of its competitors.

The real breakthrough came when Stork's team focused more closely on the RV market, which was just then beginning to explode. The point wasn't to sell more refrigerators to the RV segment; the company's market share within that segment was already nearly 100%. Rather, it was to add other products to the Dometic line, such as air-conditioning, automated awnings, generators, and systems for cooking, lighting, sanitation, and water purification. As Stork explains, "We decided to make the RV into something that you could really live in. The idea was obvious to people who knew the customers, yet it took a while to convince the manufacturers and especially the rest of our own organization." These moves fundamentally shifted the company's core. Dometic was no longer about absorption refrigeration: It was about RV interior systems and the formidable channel power gained by selling all its products through the same dealers and installers. That channel power allowed Dometic to pull off a move that enhanced its cost structure dramatically. The company streamlined its go-to-market approach in the United States by skipping a distribution layer that had always existed and approaching RV dealers directly. "We prepared for the risks like a military operation," Stork recalls, "and it was a fantastic hit. We were the only company large enough to pull this off. It let us kill off competitors faster than they could come out of the bushes." By 2005 Dometic had grown to KR 7.3 billion, or roughly U.S. $1.2 billion. No longer part of Electrolux (the private equity firm EQT bought it in 2001 and sold it to the investment firm BC Partners a few years later), the company was highly profitable and commanded 75% of the world market share for RV interior systems.

Dometic's story of growth and redefinition is especially instructive because it features all the elements we've seen repeatedly across the successful core-redefining companies we've studied. These are: (1) gradualism during transformation, (2) the discovery and use of hidden assets, (3) underlying leadership economics central to the strategy, and (4) a move from one repeatable formula that is unique to the company to another. "Gradualism" refers to the fact that Dometic never made anything like a "bet the company" move—often tempting when a business is on the ropes, but almost always a loser's game. As in the other cases of strategic renewal we studied, it redefined its core business by shifting its center of gravity along an existing vector of growth. To do this, it relied on hidden assets—resources or capabilities that it had not yet capitalized on. In Dometic's case, the treasure was its understanding of and access to customers in the RV market.

Leadership economics is a hallmark of almost every great strategy; when we see a situation in which the rich get richer, this is the phenomenon at work. Consider that most industries have more than six competitors, but usually more than 75% of the profit pool is captured by the top two. Of those two, the one with the greatest market power typically captures 70% of total profits and 75% of profits above the cost of capital. When Dometic focused on a defined market where it could stake out a leadership position, enormous financial benefits followed.

Its new growth formula offers the same kind of repeatability the old one did. Recall that Dometic's first focus was on applications for absorption refrigeration, which it pursued product by product, one of which was for RVs. The new formula angled off into a sequence of interior components for the RV customer base. Recently, as RV sales have slowed, Dometic has moved into interior systems for "live-in" vehicles in general, including boats and long-haul trucks.

Where Assets Hide

The importance of a company's overlooked, undervalued, or underutilized assets to its strategic regeneration cannot be overstated. In 21 of the 25 companies we examined, a hidden asset was the centerpiece of the new strategy.

Some of their stories are well known. A few years ago, a struggling Apple realized that its flair for software, user-friendly product design, and imaginative marketing could be applied to more than just computers—in particular, to a little device for listening to music. Today Apple's iPod-based music business accounts for nearly 50% of the company's revenues and 40% of profits—a new core. IBM's Global Services Group was once a tiny services and network-operations unit, not even a standalone business within IBM. By 2001 it was larger than all of IBM's hardware business and accounted for roughly two-thirds of the company's market value.

Why would well-established companies even have hidden assets? Shouldn't those assets have been put to work or disposed of long since? Actually, large, complex organizations always acquire more skills, capabilities, and business platforms than they can focus on at any one time. Some are necessarily neglected—and once they have been neglected for a while, a company's leaders often continue to ignore them or discount their value. But then something happens: Market conditions change, or perhaps the company acquires new capabilities that complement its forgotten ones. Suddenly the ugly ducklings in the backyard begin to look like swans in training.

The real question, then, is how to open management's eyes to the hidden assets in its midst. One way is to identify the richest hunting grounds. Our research suggests that hidden assets tend to fall into three categories: undervalued business platforms, untapped insights into customers, and underexploited capabilities. The exhibit "Where Does Your Future Lie?" details the types of assets we've seen exploited in each category. For a better understanding of how these assets came to light, let's look at some individual examples.

Where Does Your Future Lie?

If the core of your business is nearing depletion, the temptation may be great to venture dramatically away from it—to rely on a major acquisition, for instance, in order to establish a foothold in a new, booming industry. But the history of corporate transformation shows you're more likely to be successful if you seek change in your own backyard.

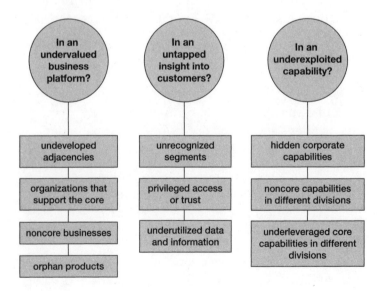

UNDERVALUED BUSINESS PLATFORMS

PerkinElmer was once the market leader in optical electronics for analytical instruments, such as spectrophotometers and gas chromatographs. Its optical capabilities were so strong that the company was chosen to manufacture the Hubble Space Telescope's mirrors and sighting equipment for NASA. Yet by 1993 PerkinElmer, its core product lines under attack by lower-cost and more innovative competitors, had stalled out. Revenues were stuck at $1.2 billion, exactly where they had been ten years earlier, and the market value of the company had eroded along with its earnings; the bottom line showed a loss of $83 million in 1993. In 1995 the board hired a new CEO, Tony White, to renew the company's strategy and performance and, if necessary, to completely redefine its core business.

As White examined the range of product lines and the customer segments served, he noticed a hidden asset that could rescue the company. In the early 1990s, PerkinElmer had branched out in another direction—developing products to amplify DNA—through a strategic alliance with Cetus Corporation. In the process, the company obtained rights to cutting-edge procedures known as polymerase chain reaction technology—a key life-sciences platform. In 1993, the company also acquired a small Silicon Valley life-sciences equipment company, Applied Biosystems (AB)—one more line of instruments to be integrated into PerkinElmer's.

White began to conceive of a redefined core built around analytical instruments for the fast-growing segment of life-sciences labs. The AB instruments in the company's catalog, if reorganized and given appropriate resources and direction, could have greater potential than even the original core. White says, "I was struck by how misconceived it was to tear AB apart and distribute its parts across the functions in the organization. I thought, 'Here is a company whose management does not see what they have.' So one of the first steps I took was to begin to reassemble the parts of AB. I appointed a new president of the division and announced that I was going to re-form the core of the company over a three-year period around this unique platform with leadership in key life-sciences detection technology."

Over the next three years, White and his team separated PerkinElmer's original core business and all the life-sciences products and services into two organizations. The employees in the analytical instruments division were given incentives to meet an aggressive cost reduction and cash flow target and told that the division would be spun off as a separate business or sold to a strong partner. Meanwhile, White set up a new data and diagnostics subsidiary, Celera Genomics, which, fueled by the passion of the scientist Craig Venter, famously went on to sequence the complete human genome. Celera and AB were combined into a new core business organization, a holding company christened Applera.

While Celera garnered the headlines, AB became the gold standard in the sequencing instrument business, with the leading market share. Today it has revenues of $1.9 billion and a healthy net income of $275 million. Meanwhile, the original instrument company was sold to the Massachusetts-based EG&G. (Soon after, EG&G changed its corporate name to PerkinElmer—and has since prospered from a combination that redefined its own core.)

The PerkinElmer-to-Applera transformation offers several lessons. The first is that a hidden asset may be a collection of products and customer relationships in different areas of a company that can be collected to form a new core. The second lesson is the power of market leadership: Finding a subcore of leadership buried in the company and building on it in a focused way created something that started smaller than the original combination but became much bigger and stronger. The third lesson lies in the concept of shrinking to grow. Though it sounds paradoxical and is organizationally difficult for companies to come to grips with, this is one of the most underused and underappreciated growth strategies. (See the insert "Shrinking to Grow" at the end of this article.)

Creating a new core based on a previously overlooked business platform is more common than one might think. General Electric, for instance, like IBM, identified an internal business unit—GE Capital—that was undervalued and underutilized. Fueled by new attention and investment, the once sleepy division made more than 170 acquisitions over a ten-year period, propelling GE's growth. By 2005 GE Capital accounted for 35% of the parent corporation's profits. Nestlé discovered that it had a number of food and drink products designed to be consumed outside the home. Like the original PerkinElmer, it assembled these products into a new unit, Nestlé Food Services; developed a unified strategy; and effectively created the core of a new multibillion-dollar business.

UNTAPPED INSIGHTS INTO CUSTOMERS

Most large companies gather considerable amounts of data about the people and businesses that buy their wares. But it's not always clear how much they actually know about those customers. In a recent series of business seminars I held for management teams, the participants took an online survey. Though nearly all came from well-regarded companies, fewer than 25% agreed with the simple statement "We understand our customers." In a 2004 Bain survey, we asked respondents to identify the most important capabilities their companies could acquire to trigger a new wave of growth. "Capabilities to understand our core customers more deeply" topped the list.

For just this reason, insights into and relationships with customers are often hidden assets. A company may discover that one neglected customer segment holds the key to unprecedented growth. It may find that it is in a position of influence over its customers, perhaps because of the trust and reputation it enjoys, and that it has not fully developed this position. Or it may find that it has proprietary data that can be used to alter, deepen, or broaden its customer relationships. All these can stimulate growth around a new core.

Harman International, a maker of high-end audio equipment, redefined its core around an unexploited customer segment. In the early 1990s it was focused primarily on the consumer and professional audio markets, with less than 10% of revenues coming from the original-equipment automotive market. But its growth had stagnated and its profits were near zero. In 1993 Sidney Harman, a cofounder, who had left the company to serve as U.S. deputy secretary of commerce, returned as CEO in an attempt to rejuvenate the company.

Harman cast a curious eye on the automotive segment. He realized that people were spending more time in their cars, and that many drivers were music lovers accustomed to high-end equipment at home. Hoping to beef up the company's sales in this sector, he acquired

the German company Becker, which supplied radios to
Mercedes-Benz. One day when Harman was visiting their
plant, some Becker engineers demonstrated how new
digital hardware allowed the company to create high-
performance audio equipment in a much smaller space
than before. That, Harman says, was the turning point.
He invested heavily in digital to create branded high-end
automotive "infotainment" systems. The systems proved
to have immense appeal both for car buyers and for car
manufacturers, who enjoyed healthy margins on the
equipment. Based largely on its success in the automotive market, Harman's market value increased 40-fold
from 1993 to 2005.

It is somewhat unusual, of course, to find an untapped
customer segment that is poised for such rapid growth.
But it isn't at all unusual for a company to discover that
its relationships with customers are deeper than it realized, or that it has more knowledge about customers
than it has put to work. Hyperion Solutions, a producer
of financial software, was able to reinvent itself around
new products and a new sales-and-service platform precisely because corporate finance departments had come
to depend on its software for financial consolidation and
SEC reporting. "We totally underestimated how much
they relied upon us for this very technical and sensitive
part of their job," says Jeff Rodek, formerly Hyperion's
CEO and now the executive chairman. American Express
transformed its credit-card business on the basis of
previously unutilized knowledge of how different customer segments used the cards and what other products
might appeal to them. Even De Beers, long known for its
monopolistic practices in the diamond industry, recently
redefined its core around consumer and customer
relationships. De Beers, of course, had long-standing

relationships with everyone in the industry. When its competitive landscape changed with the emergence of new rivals, De Beers leaders Nicky Oppenheimer and Gary Ralfe decided to make the company's strong brand and its unique image and relationships the basis of a major strategic redefinition. The company liquidated 80% of its inventory—the stockpile that had allowed it for so long to stabilize diamond prices—and created a new business model. It built up its brand through advertising. It developed new product ideas for its distributors and jewelers, and sponsored ad campaigns to market them to consumers. As a result, the estimated value of De Beers's diamond business increased nearly tenfold. The company is still in the business of selling rough diamonds, but its core is no longer about controlling supply—it's about serving consumers and customers.

UNDEREXPLOITED CAPABILITIES

Hidden business platforms and hidden customer insights are assets that companies already possess; in theory, all that remains is for management to uncover them and put them to work. Capabilities—the ability to perform specific tasks over and over again—are different. Any capability is potentially available to any company. What matters is how individual companies combine multiple capabilities into "activity systems," as Michael Porter calls them, meaning combinations of business processes that create hard-to-replicate competitive advantage. IKEA's successful business formula, Porter argued in his 1996 HBR article "What Is Strategy?," can be traced to a strong and unique set of linked capabilities, including global sourcing, design for assembly, logistics, and cost management.

An underexploited capability, therefore, can be an engine of growth if and only if it can combine with a company's other capabilities to produce something distinctly new and better. Consider the Danish company Novozymes, now a world leader in the development and production of high-quality enzymes. When it was spun off from its parent corporation in 2000, Novozymes was still largely dependent on relatively low-tech commodity enzymes such as those used in detergents.

Steen Riisgaard, the company's chief executive, set out to change that, and the key was Novozymes's under-utilized scientific capability. Riisgaard focused the company's R&D on the creation of bioengineered specialty enzymes. Its scientists worked closely with customers in order to design the enzymes precisely to their specifications. If a customer wanted to remove grease stains from laundry at unusually low temperatures, for instance, Novozymes would collect possible enzyme-producing microorganisms from all over the world, determine which one produced the enzyme closest to what was needed, remove the relevant gene, and insert the gene into an organism that could safely be produced at high volume. Riisgaard likens the process to finding a needle in a haystack, except that Novozymes uses state-of-the-art technology to single out the haystacks and accelerate the search. Such capabilities have shortened product development from five years to two and have set Novozymes apart from its competitors.

Of course, a company may find that it needs to acquire new capabilities to complement those it already has before it can create a potent activity system. Apple indisputably capitalized on its strengths in design, brand management, user interface, and elegant, easy-to-use software in creating the iPod. But it also needed expertise in the music business and in digital rights management. Once it had those, Apple gained access to content by signing up the top four recording companies before competitors could and developing the iTunes Music Store. It also created a brilliantly functional approach to digital rights management with its Fairplay software, which ensures that the music companies obtain a highly controllable revenue stream. This combination of existing and new capabilities proved transformational for Apple.

The highest form of capability development is to create a unique set of capabilities—no longer hidden—that can build one growth platform after another, repeatedly giving a company competitive advantage in multiple markets. Though difficult, this is a strong temptation; indeed, it has proved to be a siren song for many. But a few companies, such as Emerson Electric, Valspar, Medtronic, and Johnson & Johnson, have managed to avoid the rocks. A lesser-known example is Danaher, which only 20 years ago was a midsize company with $617 million in revenues and almost all its business concentrated in industrial tool markets. Danaher developed a set of procedures whereby it can identify acquisitions and then add value to the acquired companies through the so-called Danaher Business System. The system has several phases and dimensions, including cultural values, productivity improvement, sourcing techniques, and a distinctive approach to measurement and control. It has allowed Danaher to expand into six strategic platforms and 102 subunits spanning a wide range of industrial applications, from electronic testing to environmental services. The company's stock price has risen by more than 5,000% since 1987, outpacing the broader market by a factor of more than five.

It's somewhat maddening how the assets explored here—PerkinElmer's undervalued business platform, Harman's untapped customer insights, Novozymes's underexploited capabilities—can be so obvious in hindsight and yet were so hard to appreciate at the time. Will you be any better able to see what is under your nose? One thing seems clear: Your next core business will not announce itself with fanfare. More likely, you will arrive at it by a painstaking audit of the areas outlined in this article.

The first step is simply to shine a light on the dark corners of your business and identify assets that are candidates for a new core. Once identified, these assets must be assessed. Do they offer the potential of clear,

Seven Steps to a New Core Business

1. Define the core of your business.
   Reach consensus on the true state of the core.

2. Assess the core's full potential and the durability of its key differentiation.

3. Develop a point of view about the future, and define the status quo.

4. Identify the full range of options for redefining the core from the inside and from the outside.

5. Identify your hidden assets, and ask whether they create new options or enable others.

6. Use key criteria (leadership, profit pool, repeatability, chances of implementation) in deciding which assets to employ in redefining your core.

7. Set up a program office to help initiate, track, and manage course corrections.

measurable differentiation from your competition? Can
they provide tangible added value for your customers? Is
there a robust profit pool that they can help you target?
Can you acquire the additional capabilities you may need
to implement the redefinition? Like the four essentials of
a good golf swing, each of these requirements sounds
easily met; the difficulty comes in meeting all four at
once. Apple's iPod-based redefinition succeeded precisely because the company could answer every question
in the affirmative. A negative answer to any one of them
would have torpedoed the entire effort.

A Growing Imperative for Management

Learning to perform such assessments and to take gradual, confident steps toward a new core business is
increasingly central to the conduct of corporate management. Look, for example, at the fate of the *Fortune* 500
companies in 1994. A research team at Bain found that a
decade later 153 of those companies had either gone
bankrupt or been acquired, and another 130 had engi-
neered a fundamental shift in their core business strategy. In other words, nearly six out of ten faced serious
threats to their survival or independence during the
decade, and only about half of this group were able to
meet the threat successfully by redefining their core
business.

Why do so many companies face the need to transform themselves? Think of the cycle that long-lived companies commonly go through: They prosper first by
focusing relentlessly on what they do well, next by
expanding on that core to grow, and then, when the core
has lost its relevance, by redefining themselves and

focusing anew on a different core strength. It seems clear that this focus-expand-redefine cycle has accelerated over the decades. Companies move from one phase to another faster than they once did. The forces behind the acceleration are for the most part well known. New technologies lower costs and shorten product life cycles. New competitors—currently in China and India—shake up whole industries. Capital, innovation, and management talent flow more freely and more quickly around the globe. The churn caused by all this is wide-ranging. The average holding period for a share of common stock has declined from three years in the 1980s to nine months today. The average life span of companies has dropped from 14 years to just over ten, and the average tenure of CEOs has declined from eight years a decade ago to less than five today.

Business leaders are acutely aware of these waves of change and their ramifications. In 2004 my colleagues and I surveyed 259 senior executives around the world about the challenges they faced. More than 80% of them indicated that the productive lives of their strategies were getting shorter. Seventy-two percent believed that their leading competitor would be a different company in five years. Sixty-five percent believed that they would need to restructure the business model that served their primary customers. As the focus-expand-redefine cycle continues to pick up speed, each year will find more companies in that fateful third phase, where redefinition is essential. For most, the right way forward will lie in assets that are hidden from view—in neglected businesses, unused customer insights, and latent capabilities that, once harnessed, can propel new growth.

Shrinking to Grow

WHEN A COMPANY uncovers an underutilized source of leadership economics, sometimes the best response is to "double down" on its investment in that area. A bold version of this is actually shrinking to grow. Consider the example of Royal Vopak.

If you are not in the oil or chemicals business, you may not be familiar with Vopak, but it is the world leader in independent tank storage of bulk oil and chemicals, operating in 75 port locations from Rotterdam to Houston to Singapore. Vopak traces its roots back to a time when the Netherlands was the wealthiest and most powerful country in the world, owing to its role as a center for shipping and trade with the Far East. The origins of Vopak lie in a company that was founded in 1616, by a group of porters on the docks of Amsterdam, for the purpose of loading and unloading ship cargoes.

By 2000 Vopak was enjoying sales of €5.6 billion, with positions in shipping, chemical distribution, and port storage facilities. Its storage business was the most profitable. When Vopak's profits suffered and its stock price came under severe pressure, plummeting from €25 per share in June 1999 to €12 in July 2002, the company took decisive action. It spun off everything but the storage business, reducing the sales volume of the company to €750 million. But Vopak did not stop there: It even sold some of its storage portfolio, further reducing its size.

What was the result? Amazingly, the company's market value increased beyond its original level, as the stock price rebounded to €30 in May 2006. Furthermore, the stronger, well-funded business began to grow again—both organically and through acquisitions and new port locations. During the first half of 2006, Vopak's revenues grew by 17% and its earnings by 28%, in an inherently low-growth industry. John Paul Broeders, the chairman of the executive board, says, "Without shrinking first, we would never have created the resources, the management focus, and a stable platform to begin to grow again as we have."

Shrink-to-grow strategies are not an end in themselves, but they can pave the way for redefinition. These moves have a very high success rate when it comes to increasing a company's value and liberating one of the cores to strengthen and grow, provided it's given additional resources. Indeed, another three of our 25 case studies in successful core redefinition relied on this tactic: PerkinElmer, Samsung, and GUS.

Originally published in April 2007.
Reprint R0704D

From Spare Change to Real Change: The Social Sector as Beta Site for Business Innovation

ROSABETH MOSS KANTER

Executive Summary

CORPORATIONS ARE CONTINUALLY looking for new sources of innovation. Today several leading companies are beginning to find inspiration in an unexpected place: the social sector. That includes public schools, welfare-to-work programs, and the inner city.

Indeed, a new paradigm for innovation is emerging: a partnership between private enterprise and public interest that produces profitable and sustainable change for both sides.

In this article, the author shows how some companies are moving beyond corporate social responsibility to corporate social innovation. Traditionally, companies viewed the social sector as a dumping ground for their spare cash, obsolete equipment, and tired executives. But that mind-set hardly created lasting change. Now companies are viewing community needs as opportunities to develop ideas and demonstrate business technologies; find and serve new markets; and solve long-standing business problems. They focus on inventing sophisticated solutions through a hands-on approach. This is not charity; it is R&D, a strategic business investment.

The author concedes that it isn't easy to make the new paradigm work. But she has found that successful private-public partnerships share six characteristics: a clear business agenda, strong partners committed to change, investment by both parties, rootedness in the user community, links to other organizations, and a commitment to sustain and replicate the results. Drawing on examples of successful companies such as IBM and Bell Atlantic, the author illustrates how this paradigm has produced innovations that have both business and community payoffs.

W INNING IN BUSINESS today demands innovation. Companies that innovate reap all the advantages of a first mover. They acquire a deep knowledge of new markets and develop strong relationships within them. Innovators also build a reputation of being able to solve the most challenging problems. That's why corporations spend billions of dollars each year trying to identify opportunities for innovation—unsolved problems or unmet needs, things that don't fit or don't work. They set up learning laboratories where they can stretch their thinking, extend their capabilities, experiment with new technologies, get feedback from early users about product potential, and gain experience working with underserved and emerging markets.

Today several leading companies are beginning to find inspiration in an unexpected place: the social sector—in public schools, welfare-to-work programs, and the inner city. These companies have discovered that social problems are economic problems, whether it is the need for a trained workforce or the search for new markets in neglected parts of cities. They have learned that applying their energies to solving the chronic problems of the social sector powerfully stimulates their own business development. Today's better-educated children are tomorrow's knowledge workers. Lower unemployment in the inner city means higher consumption in the inner city. Indeed, a new paradigm for innovation is emerging: a partnership between private enterprise and public interest that produces profitable and sustainable change for both sides.

The new paradigm is long overdue. Traditional solutions to America's recalcitrant social ills amount to little more than Band-Aids. Consider the condition of public education. Despite an estimated 200,000 business partnerships with public schools, fundamental aspects of public education have barely changed in decades. And performance is still weak. There are two reasons for this. First, traditional corporate volunteer activities only scratch the surface. And second, companies often just throw money at the problem, then walk away. The fact is, many recipients of business largesse often don't need charity; they need change. Not spare change, but real change—sustainable, replicable, institutionalized change that transforms their schools, their job prospects, and their neighborhoods. And that means getting business deeply involved in nontraditional ways.

Doing Good by Doing Well

My team of researchers and I have found a number of companies that are breaking the mold—they are moving beyond corporate social *responsibility* to corporate social *innovation*. These companies are the vanguard of the new paradigm. They view community needs as opportunities to develop ideas and demonstrate business technologies, to find and serve new markets, and to solve long-standing business problems. They focus their efforts on inventing sophisticated solutions through a hands-on approach. (See the insert "Why America Needs Corporate Social Innovation" at the end of this article.)

Tackling social sector problems forces companies to stretch their capabilities to produce innovations that have business as well as community payoffs. When companies approach social needs in this way, they have a stake in the problems, and they treat the effort the way they would treat any other project central to the company's operations. They use their best people and their core skills. This is not charity; it is R&D—a strategic business investment. Let's look at a few examples from the fields of education, welfare programs, and inner-city development.

PUBLIC EDUCATION

In 1991, Bell Atlantic began creating one of the first-ever models for using computer networks in public schools. Bell Atlantic's Project Explore, in Union City, New Jersey, enabled communication and learning to move beyond the classroom. In addition to installing computers in the schools, Bell Atlantic gave computers to 135 inner-city students and their teachers to use at home. Project Explore became a catalyst for increasing the use of technology to transform middle- and high-school classrooms, to improve students' skills, and to involve parents in their children's education. Union City's schools, once threatened with state takeover, have become national role models. For its part, Bell Atlantic has found new ways of handling data transmission. It refined its goals for video on demand and identified a new market in distance learning.

IBM began its Reinventing Education program in 1994 under the personal leadership of CEO Louis V. Gerstner, Jr. Today the program, designed to develop new tools and solutions for systemic change, operates in 21 U.S. sites and in four other countries. Many product innovations, which benefit both the schools and IBM, have resulted from this initiative. As part of the Wired for Learning program in four new schools in Charlotte-Mecklenburg, North Carolina, for example, IBM created tools to connect parents to teachers digitally so that parents can view their children's schoolwork from home or a community center and compare it with the district's academic standard. New tracking software is facilitating the introduction of flexible scheduling in Cincinnati, Ohio, including in a new year-round high school. In Broward County, Florida—the fifth largest school district in the United States—IBM's data-warehousing technology gives teachers and administrators access to extensive information on students. In Philadelphia, Pennsylvania, IBM created a voice recognition tool to teach reading, which is based on children's high-pitched voices and speech patterns.

WELFARE-TO-WORK PROGRAMS

Since 1991, the hotel group Marriott International has been refining its pioneering training program, Pathways to Independence. The program, which currently runs in 13 U.S. cities, hones the job skills, life skills, and work habits of welfare recipients, and Marriott guarantees participants a job offer when they complete the program. The challenges of working with the unemployed has led the company to new insights about training, job placement, and supervision, which have helped Marriott reap the benefits of a more stable workforce and maintain unusually high standards of service. Pathways was a radical improvement on traditional programs for the hard to employ, which were both bureaucratically cumbersome and often ineffective. The employee assistance innovations that Marriott has developed through the program have also created new jobs in poor communities.

United Airlines is another company that derives business benefits from tapping a new workforce. Taking a leadership role in the Welfare-to-Work Partnership (a national coalition of 8,000 businesses that have pledged to hire people off the welfare rolls), CEO Gerald Greenwald seeks new ways to transport people from inner cities to suburban jobs. United has also created human resources innovations, such as a new mentoring program. These innovations, developed in collaboration with workers, have become models for the new personnel practices United is now planning to roll out to its more than 10,000 new hires.

INNER-CITY DEVELOPMENT

BankBoston launched First Community Bank in 1990 as a way to target newcomers to the banking system—many of whom were located in the inner city. This initiative also responded to regulatory pressures on banks to increase investment in underserved urban neighborhoods. Thanks to First Community Bank, access to high-quality financial services for disadvantaged minorities and inner-city inhabitants has radically improved, which is helping to revitalize deteriorating neighborhoods. Since its inception, First Community Bank has been a laboratory for a stream of innovations that have been applied across BankBoston. From BankBoston's perspective, First Community Bank has been an undeniable success. The bank has grown from its initial 7 branches in Boston to 42 branches across New England. It offers a range of products and services that includes consumer lending, real estate, small-business loans, and venture capital. Today it is the anchor for all community-banking services within BankBoston.

Making Partnerships Work

Making the new paradigm work isn't easy. In contrast to typical business-to-business relationships, there is an added layer of complexity. Government and nonprofit organizations are driven by goals other than profitability, and they may even be suspicious of business motivations. Additionally, the institutional infrastructure of the social sector is undeveloped in business terms. For that reason, public schools and inner cities can be said to resemble emerging markets. Those difficulties, however, can be overcome. My research has identified six characteristics of successful private-public partnerships: a clear business agenda, strong partners committed to change, investment by both parties, rootedness in the user community, links to other community organizations, and a long-term commitment to sustain and replicate the results.

A CLEAR BUSINESS AGENDA

In the new paradigm, companies obviously want to make a social contribution. But a corporation has a better chance of making a real difference if it knows clearly, in advance, how its business agenda relates to specific social needs. A company that wants to develop new data analysis technology, for example, might target a large and complex education system as its beta site. Finding test users in the public schools would clearly benefit both the community and the company. Indeed, apart from the social benefits, there are two distinct business advantages. The first is the opportunity to test the new technology, and the second is the chance to build political capital—for instance, to influence regulations, to reshape public institutions on which the company depends, to augment a public image as a leader, or to build closer relationships with government officials.

This coincidence of social needs with business and political goals is precisely illustrated by Bell Atlantic's Project Explore. Bell Atlantic was developing intelligent network technologies, video on demand, and other communications ideas. By the early 1990s, Bell Atlantic was ready to test High-bit-rate Digital Subscriber Line (HDSL) technologies with personal computers. Bell Communications Research, then the R&D laboratory shared by the Baby Bells after their divestiture from AT&T, sent Bell Atlantic a proposal to equip schools with computers. That would get the technology out into the field and allow the company to test the services that could be delivered over high-capacity lines into schools and homes.

Working with schools also fit the company's political agenda. In New Jersey, Bell Atlantic leaders hoped to win the support of legislators and regulators for the Opportunity New Jersey project, Bell Atlantic's proposed statewide technology communications plan. To garner support, they needed a demonstration site to showcase their communications networks. Bell Atlantic saw that testing its transmission technology in special-needs school districts could benefit both the company and the schools. Bell Atlantic's new technology, however, could work only for distances of about 9,000 feet on copper telephone wires, which in New Jersey had not yet been replaced with fiber-optic lines. The density of Union City's population and Union City's proximity to Bell Atlantic's central switching office made it an ideal site for testing and developing the company's innovations.

Marriott International also had a clear business agenda that addressed a social need. Over two-thirds of the company's 131,000 employees are entry level, lower-wage workers in housekeeping, engineering, security, maintenance, food service, and reservations. Developing an effective method to recruit, train, and retain workers in these positions has always been a critical concern. Throughout the 1980s, Marriott had reached out to untapped pockets of the labor market, such as Vietnam veterans, ex-offenders, the disabled, recent immigrants, and welfare mothers. Although the company received tax credits as a financial incentive, Marriott continued to be plagued by a high level of turnover and poor job performance. By the beginning of the 1990s, the company badly needed new sources of reliable labor. After some experimentation, the first viable Pathways program was launched in Atlanta, Georgia, in 1991. Since then, Marriott has not only reduced turnover rates but also improved job prospects in inner cities.

STRONG PARTNERS COMMITTED TO CHANGE

A critical feature of the new paradigm is the presence
of committed social sector organizations and leaders
who are already working on change. These can include
public servants and community figures such as mayors,
governors, school superintendents, and civic activists.
Companies need such partners to bring together diverse
constituencies and to provide political legitimacy. Strong
support helps ensure that new solutions will create systemic change, not languish in isolated projects. Committed social partners can also help businesses win access
to underserved markets—for example, the inner city—
and they can build widespread support for other new
ventures.

Consider how IBM chose partners for its Reinventing
Education initiative. The company singled out school
districts where leaders were thinking in new and
creative ways. When evaluating grant proposals, IBM
looked for widely communicated education reform goals
and strategic plans that clearly identified where projects
could add value. The backing of strong mayors who
were personally committed to education reform was
considered vital. Mayor Edward Rendell, for example,
supported superintendent David Hornbeck's program,
Children Achieving in Philadelphia. The program
showed how business involvement could contribute
and was a major factor behind IBM's decision to invest
there. Similarly, in Florida, Broward County's nine-point
vision statement and five-year information technology
plan were crucial in convincing IBM to get involved. By
seizing on local agendas, IBM ensured that its projects
would command the personal attention of superintendents and other key figures.

Bell Atlantic also found willing partners already working on major change. A key factor in getting Project Explore started was the commitment of Thomas Highton, superintendent of schools, and Congressman Robert Menendez, then state senator and mayor of Union City. When Highton was promoted to superintendent in 1988, Union City schools were failing on almost all scores. There was very little teacher involvement in decision making or parent involvement in their children's education; facilities were in poor shape; the curriculum was outdated; there was little to no technology. Highton proposed to turn an abandoned parochial school into a technology school, an action that required state approval. For his part, Menendez wanted to get fiber-optic networks throughout New Jersey to improve education and health services. Bell Atlantic's proposal was timely. The company's commitment to Union City, brokered by Menendez, gave Highton the credibility he needed to get approval to buy the abandoned parochial school. The school was renamed after Christopher Columbus to reflect the journey of discovery ahead in the trial called Project Explore.

Partners for educational projects are easily identifiable because schools are large and highly organized. Companies confronting other social needs, however, may encounter many small nonprofit organizations, each of which works on a different piece of the problem. Marriott worked with various government and nonprofit partners in each of its Pathways to Independence programs— organizations such as Goodwill Industries, the Jewish Vocational Service, Private Industry Councils, and Workforce Development Boards. Marriott chose the strongest partner in each community.

United Airlines was also confronted with a patchwork of small community organizations working with welfare recipients. In launching its welfare-to-work efforts in San Francisco, United chose one strong nonprofit placement organization to be its lead partner and urged other groups to work through that agency. The details differ, but in all cases, strong partnerships are a crucial aspect of the new paradigm.

INVESTMENT BY BOTH PARTIES

The best way to ensure full commitment is to have both partners—not just the corporate but the community partner—put their resources on the line. Investment by both partners builds mutuality. It also ensures that the community partner will sustain the activities when contributions from business taper off.

In all of IBM's Reinventing Education initiatives, both partners put their hands in their pockets. IBM gave each school system a $2 million grant—up to 25% in cash and 75% or more in technical equipment, software, research, and consulting time. The team at each site determined the mix. Almost all of IBM's grant to Broward County, for example, went toward consulting time.

The schools also contributed financially to the projects, both in the development phase and when full rollout took place after the money ran out. The Philadelphia school system, for example, bought at least 109 computers in addition to the 36 PCs and 8 ThinkPads provided by IBM. Individual school principals also supplemented IBM and central office funds from their own budgets. To help manage the transition to internal leadership in Broward County, for instance, the schools paid for an IBM project manager and systems architect to remain for several months after grant funds were expended. Each school district also used considerable funds on staff time for planning and training, in addition to major technology investments.

BankBoston and its community partners sometimes share the costs of First Community Bank's projects. In Hartford, Connecticut, First Community Bank worked with the South Hartford Initiative, a community development organization, to establish a unique small-business lending program in 1997. That innovation took many months to structure and negotiate. First Community Bank funds an average of 46% of each loan in South Hartford Initiative's neighborhoods; SHI funds the balance on a fully subordinated basis. First Community Bank reduces its normal commitment fee and interest rate, and SHI agrees to collect only interest for the term of the loan, until the principal amount is due. SHI has the option to underwrite loans declined by the bank, and First Community then services those loans.

Investment by both parties means more than just financial investments. Consider the Pathways to Independence program. Some of Marriott's partners make direct financial contributions: Goodwill Industries reimburses over half of the program's costs of approximately $5,000 per student in those cities in which it is Marriott's partner. But even partners that don't contribute financially commit resources. For example, while Marriott provides uniforms, lunches, training sites, program management, on-the-job training, and mentoring, its partners help locate and screen candidates and assist them with housing, child care, and transportation.

During the life of an innovation project, the balance of investments can shift. Bell Atlantic bore the bulk of the costs for Project Explore when it was launched in 1993, after two years of planning. The company wired the new Columbus Middle School; trained the teachers; and gave

135 seventh graders and their teachers computers in their homes, along with printers and access to the Internet. Once involved, Bell Atlantic found its commitment growing. Even when the project had moved beyond a trial phase and had to compete for company resources every year, Bell Atlantic kept a project team on board to follow the group through seventh and eighth grades and into Emerson High. By 1995, Union City began to pick up the bills. The school system received a National Science Foundation grant to wire Emerson High School and buy most of the computers. By 1997, Union City was picking up 100% of the cost, although a part-time project manager from Bell Atlantic's Opportunity New Jersey remained to maintain the relationship.

Both partners also need to make strong staff commitments. IBM ensures that responsibilities in this area are balanced: a school-district project sponsor is matched with an IBM project executive, and a school district project manager with an IBM on-site project manager. IBM does not rely on volunteers or part-time staff. It recruits the best talent it can for assignments, which are considered challenging as well as personally rewarding. Participants in the programs must report their monthly costs and expenses—just as they would report them to the CEO of a client company. Says an IBM official, "We treat our school partners the way we treat our best customers."

The experience of working so closely with businesses has had a deep impact on organizations in the social sector. Schools involved in the Bell Atlantic and IBM experiments, for example, have found that they have had to become more efficient and market-oriented in selecting staff for the projects.

ROOTEDNESS IN THE USER COMMUNITY

Innovation is facilitated when developers learn directly from user experience. Therefore, IBM's projects were designed to bring technologists close to the schools. In Broward County, the initial IBM office was housed in the computer lab at Sunrise Middle School. This location enabled constant interaction between IBM staff and teachers who evaluated the software. Moreover, becoming part of the school environment fostered rapid acceptance of the IBM team. "They even ate cafeteria food," an administrator exclaimed.

Yet even when a company goes on-site, there can be cultural obstacles. IBM employees tended to see school procedures as bureaucratic, while teachers had negative stereotypes of people working in large corporations. "We move at different speeds," one IBM team member explained. Cultural differences were also apparent in language—jargon was a significant barrier to communication. According to one IBM employee, the "educational world has even more acronyms than the IBM world, which surprised everybody." But over time, the presence of IBM people in the schools, and their openness to learn from educators, helped bridge the differences and allayed many of the schools' concerns that they would be taken over by businesspeople.

In the inner-city neighborhoods in which it operates, BankBoston's First Community Bank takes great care in staffing its branches to ensure that the employees understand the community. First Community Bank founder and president Gail Snowden, for example, grew up in the bank's core neighborhood, where her parents ran a well-regarded community service organization. First

Community Bank managers are expected to attend community events as part of their job. The bank has created new functions—such as community development officers who act as liaisons with customers in specific ethnic populations—to further embed it in its communities. The bank also offers customized technical assistance—for example, document translation or explanation of customs to new immigrants. Although these service innovations increase the time spent per transaction, they make First Community Bank branches part of the fabric of the neighborhood. That helps make parent BankBoston a leader in the urban market.

LINKS TO OTHER ORGANIZATIONS

For projects to succeed, the business partner must call on the expertise of key players in the broader community. Bell Atlantic, for example, brought in the Stevens Institute of Technology—which had expertise in Internet capabilities and equipment configurations—to help build a curriculum for teachers around Internet access. Similarly, IBM nurtured connections with the school districts' other partners, some of which already had a deep local presence. In Philadelphia, IBM relied on the Philadelphia Education Fund—an offshoot of Greater Philadelphia First, a coalition of the city's 35 largest corporations—as a source of local knowledge. In Cincinnati, IBM convened businesses and funders such as Procter & Gamble and General Electric to ensure that everyone worked toward the same ends in the schools.

BankBoston, too, finds its broader community and government contacts to be useful sources of additional ideas and finance for riskier deals and start startup businesses. First Community Bank's community development group, for instance, worked with about eight other banks and the U.S. Small Business Administration to create a new "fast track" SBA loan approval. Without external collaboration, no business innovation partnership can expect to enact lasting change.

A LONG-TERM COMMITMENT TO SUSTAIN AND REPLICATE THE SOLUTION

Like any R&D project, new-paradigm partnerships require sustained commitment. The inherent uncertainty of innovation—trying something that has never been done before in that particular setting—means that initial project plans are best guesses, not firm forecasts. Events beyond the company's control, unexpected obstacles in technology, political complexities, new opportunities or technologies unknown at the time plans were made—all of these can derail the best-laid plans. First Community Bank took five years to show a profit, but last year it was number one in sales out of all of BankBoston's retail operations. Investments in the social sector, just as in any start-up, require patient capital.

Each of the new-paradigm companies described wanted to create a successful prototype or demonstration project in the test site. But test sites, by nature, receive concentrated attention and resources. The real challenge is not sustaining an individual project but replicating it elsewhere. The best innovations can be mass-produced, adopted by users in other settings, and supported by additional investors. That is why replication and extension were explicit parts of IBM's strategy.

The Reinventing Education project began in ten school districts. First-round grants from IBM covered a three- to five-year period, and IBM wanted most of the money disbursed in the first two years so that the next three could be spent diffusing the innovation and examining the project's impact. Tools developed in the first round of innovations were then introduced through an additional 12 projects. To help the sites complete their individual rollouts, IBM staff continue to monitor sites for five years. IBM encourages cross-fertilization of ideas among all the Reinventing Education project sites. Broward County, for example, hosts officials from other school districts on a quarterly basis. Charlotte-Mecklenburg's Wired for Learning prototype is spreading throughout North Carolina. And an IBM Web site discussion forum also helps spread ideas among the project sites—an arrangement that is beneficial both to schools and to IBM.

How Business Benefits

Sometimes business attempts to find innovation in the social sector are discounted by critics as public relations ploys. But as the depth and breadth of each company's commitment should make clear, that would be an extremely costly and risky way to get favorable press. The extensive efforts described here, with their goal of creating systemic change, also cannot be justified only on the grounds that they make employees or the community feel good—even though that obviously motivates people to work hard. In reality, the primary business justification for the sustained commitment of resources is the new knowledge and capabilities that will stem from innovation—the lessons learned from the tough problems solved.

Bell Atlantic's Project Explore was expensive, and it was not philanthropy. It was funded out of operating and technology-development budgets. Certainly, Bell Atlantic people felt good about helping inner-city schoolchildren succeed. And the company generates a continuing and growing revenue stream from selling network services to the education market, which it learned how to approach from its extensive experience in Union City. But the ultimate business justification for Project Explore was the know-how Bell Atlantic developed about networking technologies. As John Grady, now HDSL product manager but then the first Union City project manager, puts it, "the Union City trial provided the first evidence that HDSL technology could work." In April 1997, Grady and three other Bell Atlantic employees received a patent for a public-switch telephone network for multimedia transmission—a direct consequence of the innovations developed in Union City. That patent ultimately led to the introduction of Bell Atlantic's new Infospeed DSL product line in 1999.

IBM, too, stretches its technical capabilities by tackling the difficult problems in public schools. IBM employees experimented with new technology that has commercial applications. For the Reinventing Education project in Cincinnati, for example, IBM researchers developed new drag-and-drop technology for the Internet, which uses the latest features of Java and HTML and can be leveraged throughout IBM. As a systems architect in Cincinnati remarked, "The group that I'm working with and I have learned more on this project than any other that we've worked on previously. We're working with people from the ground up. When we started, there was absolutely nothing except an idea about new Internet technology." And the Broward County project extended IBM's data-warehousing know-how from small groups of users in retailing and related industries to very large groups of users with complicated data requirements—over 10,000 teachers and administrators in a school system.

Marriott's Pathways to Independence has produced tangible benefits for the company. About 70% of Pathways' graduates are still employed by Marriott after a year, compared with only 45% of the welfare hires who did not participate in Pathways and only 50% of other new hires. Marriott estimates that program costs are recovered if graduates are retained 2.5 times longer than the average new hire. In fact, Pathways is considered to be such a source of competitive advantage for Marriott that the company shares only the general outlines of the program with other companies and keeps the details proprietary. And success in the Pathways to Independence program has encouraged Marriott to undertake other initiatives, such as the Associate Resource Line, a hot line that provides assistance with housing, transportation, immigration, financial and legal issues, even pet care. It cost Marriott $2 million to set up the hot line; it now saves $4 for every dollar spent, through lower turnover and reduced absenteeism.

BankBoston, too, has found business benefits from its social initiative. Its First Community Bank has become both a profitable operating unit and a source of product and service innovations that have been applied across all of BankBoston. These include First Step products for newcomers to banking; multilingual ATMs; a new venture-capital unit for equity investments in inner-city businesses; and community development officers, who help create lending opportunities. In fact, First Community bank has been so successful that Bank-Boston is refocusing its retail strategy toward community banking.

Employees' opinions of the initiative have also been transformed. Far from being a dead-end assignment, a position at First Community Bank is highly desirable because it offers the challenge and excitement of innovation. In January 1999, founding president Gail Snowden was promoted to head up the regional leadership group for all of BankBoston's retail banking. And in March 1999, President Clinton presented BankBoston with the Ron Brown Award for Corporate Leadership (for which I was a judge) in recognition of its community-banking activities. Clearly, businesses that partake in these new-paradigm partnerships reap tangible benefits.

Spreading the New Paradigm

This article describes a new way for companies to approach the social sector: not as an object of charity but as an opportunity for learning and business development, supported by R&D and operating funds rather than philanthropy. Traditional charity and volunteerism have an important role in society, but they are often not the best or fastest way to produce innovation or transformation.

High-impact business contributions to the social sector use the core competencies of a business—the things it does best. For Bell Atlantic, it is communications technology; for IBM, it is information technology solutions; for Marriott, it is service strategies. In this new paradigm, the activities are focused on results, seeking measurable outcomes and demonstrated changes. The effort can be sustained and replicated in other places. The community gets new approaches that build capabilities and point the way to permanent improvements. The business gets bottom-line benefits: new products, new solutions to critical problems, and new market opportunities.

New-paradigm partnerships could reinvent American institutions. They open new possibilities for solving recalcitrant social and educational problems. They give businesses a new way to innovate. Today these examples are still works in progress. But tomorrow they could be the way business is done everywhere.

Why America Needs Corporate Social Innovation

DESPITE ITS LONG economic boom, America's social problems abound. To ensure future economic success, the country needs dramatic improvement in public schools, more highly skilled workers, jobs with a future for people coming off the welfare rolls, revitalized urban centers and inner cities, and healthy communities. Traditionally, businesses have supported the social sector in two different ways: they contribute their employees' time for volunteer activities, and they support community initiatives with money and gifts in kind. Both activities can accomplish many good things and should be encouraged, but neither activity engages the unique skills and capabilities of business.

Consider the typical corporate volunteer program. It almost invariably draws on the lowest common skills in a company by mobilizing people to do physical work–landscaping a school's grounds or painting walls in a community center. Such projects are good for team building and may augment limited community budgets, even build new relationships, but they don't change the education system or strengthen economic prospects for community residents. In many cases, it is just as effective for the business simply to write a check to community residents or a small neighborhood organization to do the work.

And that, indeed, is what many companies do. A great deal of business participation in social sector problems derives from the classic model of arm's-length charity—writing a check and leaving everything else to government and nonprofit agencies. Businesses have little involvement in how these donations are used. In fact, this model actively discourages companies from taking an interest in results. Companies receive their benefits up-front through tax write-offs and the public relations boost that accompanies the announcement of their largesse. There is little or no incentive to stay involved or to take responsibility for seeing that the contribution is used to reach a goal. However well meaning, many businesses treat the social sector as a charity case—a dumping ground for spare cash, obsolete equipment, and tired executives on their way out.

Such arm's-length models of corporate philanthropy have not produced fundamental solutions to America's most urgent domestic problems of public education, jobs for the disadvantaged, and neighborhood revitalization. Nor will they, because traditional charity can't reach the root of the problems; it just treats the symptoms. Most business partnerships with schools, for example, are limited in scope: they usually provide local resources to augment a school program, such as scholarship funds, career days, sponsorship of an athletic team, or volunteer reading tutors. The criteria for involvement are minimal, often hinging only on geographic proximity to a company site. The 600 school principals I surveyed said they are grateful for any help from the business sector. But what they really want today, when public education is under attack, are new ideas for systemic change that private enterprises are uniquely qualified to contribute.

As government downsizes and the public expects the private sector to step in to help solve community problems, it is important that businesses understand why the old models of corporate support don't create sustainable change. In partnership with government and nonprofits, businesses need to go beyond the traditional models to tackle the much tougher task of innovation.

Originally published May 1999
Reprint 99306

About the Contributors

SCOTT D. ANTHONY is the managing director of Innosight, an innovation and strategy consulting firm, and a coauthor, with Clayton Christensen and Erik Roth, of *Seeing What's Next: Using the Theories of Innovation to Predict Industry Change* (Harvard Business School Press, 2004).

JOSEPH L. BOWER is the Donald Kirk David Professor of Business Administration at the Harvard Business School in Boston, Massachusetts.

CLAYTON M. CHRISTENSEN is the Robert and Jane Cizik Professor of Business Administration at Harvard Business School, with a joint appointment in Technology and Operations Management and General Management. He is the author of *The Innovator's Dilemma* and *The Innovator's Solution* for Harvard Business Press, as well as numerous other books and articles. He is also the cofounder, with Mark W. Johnson, of Innosight, an innovation and strategy consulting firm.

MATT EYRING is the managing director of Innosight Capital, an early stage investing company in Watertown, Massachusetts.

LIB GIBSON is a corporate adviser in the office of the CEO at Bell Canada Enterprises in Toronto.

VIJAY GOVINDARAJAN is the Earl C. Daum 1924 Professor of International Business at Dartmouth College's Tuck School of Business in Hanover, New Hampshire, and is the codirector, with Chris Trimble, of the William F. Achtmeyer Center for Global Leadership at Tuck. He and Trimble also coauthored *Ten Rules for Strategic Innovators: From Idea to Execution* (Harvard Business School Press, 2005).

MARK W. JOHNSON is the chairman of Innosight, an innovation and strategy consulting firm he cofounded in 2000 with Clayton M. Christensen, and author of *Seizing the White Space: Business Model Innovation for Transformative Growth and Renewal* (Harvard Business Press, 2009).

HENNING KAGERMANN is the co-CEO of SAP AG, in Walldorf, Germany.

ROSABETH MOSS KANTER is the Class of 1960 Professor of Business Administration at Harvard Business School in Boston, Massachusetts. She is the author of *World Class: Thriving Locally in the Global Economy* (Simon & Schuster, 1995) and *Rosabeth Moss Kanter on the Frontiers of Management* (Harvard Business School Press, 1997), and coeditor of *Innovation* (HarperCollins, 1997).

IAN C. MACMILLAN is the George W. Taylor Professor of Entrepreneurial Studies and professor of management at the University of Pennsylvania's Wharton School in Philadelphia.

JOAN MAGRETTA is a management consultant and writer and a past winner of HBR's McKinsey Award; her article draws on material from her book *What Management Is: How It Works, and Why It's Everyone's Business* (Free Press, 2002).

RITA GUNTHER MCGRATH is an assistant professor in the Management of Organizations Division of Columbia University's Graduate School of Business in New York City.

CHRIS TRIMBLE is an adjunct associate professor of business administration at Tuck and a senior fellow at Katzenbach Partners in New York. He is the codirector, with Vijay Govindarajan, of the William F. Achtmeyer Center for Global Leadership at Tuck. He and Govindarajan also coauthored *Ten Rules for Strategic Innovators: From Idea to Execution* (Harvard Business School Press, 2005).

CHRIS ZOOK is the author of *Unstoppable: Finding Hidden Assets to Renew the Core and Fuel Profitable Growth* (Harvard Business School Press, 2007), from which this article is adapted. Based in Amsterdam, he leads the Global Strategy Practice of Bain & Company.

Index